TESTIMONIALS

Are you a woman who is hungry for empowering strategies to help you better manage your stress and emotional highs and lows? Peta gracefully takes her readers on a powerful journey to discover and embrace the beautiful 'you' within. She will inspire you to choose confidence, make a difference and become an influencer in whichever environment God has positioned you. You will be glad you came for the ride!

> – SUZIE BOTROSS, author, speaker, learning and development consultant

Peta is a genuine person, who loves to connect with others and help them develop their gifting and confidence in God. She has travelled through the challenges of life and is able to encourage and empower others through her testimony. This book touches on parts of her journey in order to help you with yours.

> – SUE EARL, senior pastor (with husband), author, biblical lecturer and PhD candidate on Ezekiel.

Any ordinary everyday kind of woman who wants to make the most of who she is and what she contains on the inside deserves this book. Peta believes that every woman can make a difference and in this book she explains how. It is a must read!

> – DR MICHELLE SANDERS, Director: Art and Soul, Manager, Arts and Community Development, Eastern College, Victoria.

Peta is an authentic person who has lived the story and truly desires to see others shine. She inspires me to rethink my own limitations and seek God's perspective daily.

> – ANGELA (NEE FEDELE) BATTEN, former journalist for News Limited and sub-editor at Herald Sun.

Do you want to learn how to overcome
continual stress,
up-and-down emotions
and self-image insecurities that leave you feeling
frazzled and ineffective?

Then read on.

Within the three self-contained sections of this book,
there are doable step-by-step strategies
with plenty of before-and-after real-life stories
to get you started.

Putting these into your life
can bring about dramatic change
so that those in your world will notice
a significant difference.

Watch as *the ripple effect*
of beautiful influence
extends outwards from a *NEW* and dazzling *YOU!*

PETA SOORKIA

UN-FRAZZLE & RE-DAZZLE

FINDING REAL PEACE, FREEDOM & BEAUTY

WOMAN OF INFLUENCE
SERIES

© 2017, Peta Soorkia

Un-frazzle and Re-dazzle

WOMAN OF INFLUENCE series

ISBN: 978-0-9944623-2-9 (Second Edition)

First edition ISBN: 978-0-9944623-0-5 Published 2016.

Reproduction of elements of this book is allowable for non-commercial use only, but acknowledgement of authorship is required.

Cover design and internal illustrative elements:
Miriam McWilliam mimi-myrtle.com
Internal Book layout by:
Cameron Semmens www.webcameron.com

to

Mary Delilah

a woman of significant influence

about the author

Peta Soorkia is passionate about inspiring women to be all that they can be.

As a Christian women's life coach, speaker and founder of A Woman of Influence (www.awomanofinfluence.weebly.com) Peta has seen hundreds of women's lives transformed as they learn how to connect with their heavenly Father and relax. As women gain godly confidence in the person they were designed to be, change happens. They can become beautiful influencers.

Peta comes with a wealth of experience in personal styling and fashion design to help you look and dress beautifully. As an educator in communication skills, Peta can assist you to get your point across and as a former pastor, to help get to the heart of the matter.

Peta is married to David, lives in Melbourne, Australia and has two adult children.

To contact Peta for speaking or coaching go to www.petasoorkia.com.au.

(A percentage of the sales of this book go to A Woman of Influence's fundraising effort for A21 – the abolition of human trafficking in the 21st century).

a brief word from the author

This book has been written for you.

Why? Because although you may not realise this, you have influence!

And it is significant. And powerful.

The ways in which you interact with others are silently or loudly influencing the world around you. Even if you feel that you have nothing to offer, by examining yourself in the pages of this book, the real you that has been longing to burst forth with effective results can be unearthed. You can at long last have the meaningful and positive impact in your world that you were created for.

The book is unashamedly Bible-based and in it I endeavor to present practical strategies to help you deal with every woman's crazy-life stresses and deepest burdens. I also give you tips on how to unlock your inner beauty in order to glow gorgeously.

Throughout the whole book I believe that you will be encouraged as you read real-life before-and-after stories from women that I have personally walked with and as I openly share my own struggles too.

I hope in these pages that you will find in me, a friend who understands where you are at whilst simultaneously be inspired, motivated and empowered to beautifully and positively influence your world.

Get ready to be un-frazzled and re-dazzled.

– Peta

contents

Introduction: **World changing influence**

influence changes everything	1
influence, on the radio	1
making ripples	3
some bible women	5
travelling together	7
a prayer	10

Section 1. **Un-frazzled peace** — 11

1. Stress, the peace stealer — 13

interruptions to order	14
choose peace	16
peace and stress	17
motivators for change	19
stress costs	21
stress and money	23
clear thinking? forget it!	24
the emotional roller coaster	26
getting along	28
stress costs health	30
before and after	31
short and sweet	34
journey journaling	35
a prayer	36

2. Getting off the treadmill — 37

self care	38
busy isn't best	39
perfect timing	40
planning tomorrows	42
a personal recharge	44
stop doing	46
say no! Oh no!	47
what stop looks like	50

contents

how do you define rest?	50
sweet sleep	52
laugh out loud	55
God's rest and peace	56
before and after	59
short and sweet	62
journey journaling	63
a prayer	64
3. Stress less	65
a God moment	66
a touch of God	68
meditation is biblical	69
discipline and focus	71
slow your breathing!	72
dump your junk	74
being with God	76
the Lord is my shepherd	79
persevere	81
peace anywhere, anytime	82
GM tips	85
the overflow	86
before and after	89
short and sweet	90
journal the journey	91
a prayer	92
Section 2. **Un-frazzled freedom**	93
4. Freedom for starters	95
influencing well	96
courage for change	97
digging deep to be real	98
surrendering control	101

contents

	shut up self and listen	104
	God talk	107
	before and after	109
	short and sweet	111
	journey journaling	112
	a prayer	112
5. Freedom stealers		113
	life and bugs	114
	roots, fruits and those bugs	116
	the heart of the matter	117
	fear produces: living-life-afraid fruit	119
	unforgiveness produces: strife fruit	121
	pride produces: me-myself-and-I fruit	124
	judgements produce: the blame-game fruit	126
	envy and idols produces: I want more fruit	129
	self pity produces: poor-me fruit	131
	having gratitude can change the course of our lives	131
	before and after	133
	short and sweet	135
	journey journaling	136
	a prayer	136
6. Seize your freedom		137
	love, happiness and fruit	138
	an attitude of gratitude	140
	prayer and fasting? no way!	142
	feeling to healing	147

contents

feelings chart	150
why, why, why to uncover the lie	151
four Rs to freedom	152
responsibility	153
repent	154
reject	155
revelation	157
a prayer of freedom	157
the worst and the best	158
before and after	159
short and sweet	161
journal the journey	162
a prayer	163
Section 3. Dazzling influence	165
7. Beautiful inside	167
what we believe	168
flourishing	171
inside on the outside	172
God's dress sense	175
getting the beauty out	180
before and after	181
short and sweet	184
journal the journey	185
a prayer	185
8. Beautiful outside	187
help for the fashion helpless	188
looking your best	188
undressed	190
shape up	191
the hourglass	192
the rectangle	193

contents

	the inverted triangle	193
	the triangle	194
	some shape tips	195
	a world of colour	196
	cool baby cool	199
	warm and cuddly	199
	some colour tips	200
	your wardrobe sorted	201
	some dressing tips	205
	dressing speaks	207
	before and after	208
	short and sweet	211
	journey journalling	212
	a prayer	213
9. The best influence		215
	let it flow	216
	a love waltz	218
	a prayer	219
Appendices		221
Endnotes		230
Acknowledgements		238

Un-frazzle & Re-dazzle

INTRODUCTION:
WORLD CHANGING INFLUENCE

influence changes everything

How do you influence? By living life to the full and sharing the overflow of that to others? Or living life with a long crabby face as a result of the inner heart issues and spreading that around instead? Personally I walked a million miles with a sour heart and that story will unfold through the pages of this book as I describe inner transformation that is possible for all of us.

Perhaps like me you have lived grumpy too. In some way or other, we are all exerting some sort of effect, good or bad, often without realising it...in positive or less-than-positive ways. When we smile, when we encourage or when we feel low, we're impacting others in some way. If we take time to develop our inner well-being then we can build and inspire to bring life to others as we outwork what God originally intended for us. We were created at this time and place for a purpose[1] to influence well. And even when we do positively affect others sometimes we don't realise or appreciate our strengths.

influence, on the radio

I was feeling extremely disappointed but resigned, over a recent message I had given to a group of women. In my mind it should have, could have been sooooo much better. I didn't expect to be another Joyce Meyer (a hard act to follow), or a Christine Caine (A21 & Hillsong). So, I decided dejectedly, I'll just be what I am, an average and ordinary speaker.

I turned on the radio to listen to my favourite Christian radio station to boost my spirits as I drove to the gym. I had organised myself earlier than usual that morning. The friend I had agreed to pick up had cancelled out at the last minute.

The station was in fundraising mode. The announcer introduced a listener whose life had been impacted and touched by the station's programming to encourage others to donate. I was surprised that the listener-speaker was also named Peta (we are few in number), and as I know personally of one other who is Christian, I listened carefully to discover if it was her.

Her words encouraged and inspired me as I observed what an articulate and great speaker she was. I was convicted to give a donation.

As I listened I found myself agreeing with everything she was saying and thought, that's exactly what I think and would similarly say myself! In fact, it's so alike to my experiences and how I feel … ! And then the penny dropped.

It was me! Yes, me speaking. Taped some years ago, I was now listening to that recording of me speaking over the radio at the exact time that I really needed to hear it. When I was feeling unhappy about my abilities. I believe God was telling me, that through Him, I am an anointed speaker as I encourage and influence others in my un-Joyce, un-Christine, true-to-Peta way. Tears fell as I remembered the unusual time of driving on that exact day with the radio on instead of chatting with my friend as I would have if she had been with me. I had been well and truly set up in a wonderful way, to have my confidence boosted by my

introduction

loving God. Hey, I was so motivated by my words that I pulled over to ring the station to give!

That's influence.

You may not believe this at the moment but by the end of this book I hope that you will believe deep in your soul that you carry something remarkable within to distribute to others. Just as I didn't think I had a gift, and God showed me loud and clear that I do, so do you. In the same way, your gifts do not need to be compared with those of other people because you are of worth and important in your own individual way.

In fact if you are living and breathing and on the planet, you are here for good reason. Realizing your incredible significance and what you contain is a journey of discovery that might take some effort. But let me assure you it will be well worth the trouble at the end of your journey.

You are on that journey here. You have something precious to share with others in your world and from you the extraordinary is possible.

making ripples

People the world over are looking for something to complete them and it's our incredible destiny, yours and mine, to represent God, who is the only true source of fulfilment. Each of us contains something special, unique, different, maybe even quirky that can point to God's creative power. Even your peculiarities have a part to play in His plan for you and those in your life. He created you for a specific purpose, warts and all, to change your world in small ways and subsequently, the world beyond. Influence is exercising power, affecting others' thinking[2], actions and potentially changing history itself!

If we as women take up the challenge to develop, grow and celebrate who we are, we could literally change the world in ways we may not believe possible.

There is one condition to growth. We must choose it. God is gentle to lead us but I have been known to yelp, and scream, 'ouch, no' when I'm learning against my preferred way! You heard my screams! Believe it or not, no matter how ill-prepared you and I might feel, God has all the resources we need if we could and would only access Him.

Just imagine with me if you will, regularly being able to connect with the God of this universe. You'd be different, right? The God Who, in the middle of your busy, challenging, and sometimes impossible circumstances, could fill you up like a tap pouring life-giving liquid into you, a thirsty, empty waiting vessel.

Perhaps you can see yourself as a beautifully crafted container that God fills, full-to-overflowing in order to pour out to others in your world. Can you see it? Imagine that this continually overflowing treasury is continually pouring into a far-reaching pool representing your life and your world. And this transfer produces ripples as each drop touches your pool, which is your immediate world, to create ever-widening circles of ripples and influence.

Think of yourself already, today, a ripple maker. You can beautifully influence others from where you've been placed. Wherever you go, whatever you say and do, ripples are extending outwards from you, the pouring vessel. Whether you are making a splash or a small drip-by-drip deposit, the ripples affect your husband, children, parents, siblings, close friends and acquaintances and then their ripples reach further and wider.

Your pool. Your world – out to the edges of your pool and then further to a world beyond.

There are men and women today, and in history, who affected change in their world making it a different place. Let's look at a couple now and then some women from Bible history.

Pastors Brian and Bobbie Houston are ripple makers. From a small church beginning just over 30 years ago, Hillsong is now known around the world for lively and stirring worshipful songs. But it's not just the music. It's the man, the woman whose life desires and commitments are to love God and love people. I'm totally inspired by the heart of this couple to touch lives, to love God, to lift and support the church. Not just Hillsong, but the church. Ripple makers extraordinaire, Christ's body. There are many well-known and unsung heroes of the church, doing what they can and what they are meant to do.

You may know some influential ripple makers yourself. Perhaps you look at these superheroes and compare your life to theirs, thinking that you don't have what it takes to do anything of significance. On the contrary, all of us have miraculous potential.

We can learn some great lessons about impacting others, both positively or not, by looking at some Bible women

some bible women

The whole world has been influenced by Eve. As the first woman, Eve was created to complete man, Adam. I think that's pretty amazing. What a destiny she was starting for all of us ladies, as the mother of all mankind. What a promise was hers and is ours! Just like her we are filled with promise, but, as women, we want more.

Influenced by the deceiver, she ate and then got Adam in on the action – eating from the forbidden fruit from the only tree in the garden that was off limits.

> *... She also gave to her husband with her, and he ate.*³

Whoops! The rest is history. Influence spreads. For good, order and love or for disorder, trouble and discord. But, let's not judge Eve, as God's grace was available then for her as it is today through Christ for you and me.

Esther also influenced. She affected the world by rescuing a nation that in a later age birthed the Saviour of the world. That's some influence, and beautiful at that. Producing what's good. Esther listened to wise and godly counsel from her cousin and chose to do an unselfish act at a high cost – that of possibly losing her life!

> *If you keep quiet at a time like this ... you and your relatives will die. Who knows if perhaps you were made queen for just such a time as this? Then Esther sent this reply to Mordecai: Go and gather together all the Jews of Susa and fast for me. Do not eat or drink for three days, night or day. My maids and I will do the same. And then, though it is against the law, I will go in to see the king. If I must die, I must die.*⁴

Esther encouraged a whole nation to fast and pray, as she mobilised those around her. As the story unfolds she used her beautiful and strong influence with the king to change the fate of the Jewish race and subsequently the whole world! That's some powerful sway in anyone's language.

Abigail was also a woman of strong influence. She was not only beautiful, but also discerning, sensible, intelligent with good judgement – I like this girl!

> *... Nabal ... wife's name was Abigail. She was an intelligent and beautiful woman ...*⁵

Abigail decisively saved her people from David's angry response to her husband Nabal's bad decision. Nabal foolishly and rudely refused to assist David's hungry men. Abigail wisely intercepted David's men sending an apology and food. (What do they say about the way to a man's heart?) Something worked, because David was so impressed with both Abigail's beauty and wisdom, that the tribe was saved from David's vengeance.

May you be blessed for your good judgment ...[6]

Later after Nabal's untimely death (or timely, for Abigail), David made her his wife.

She was elevated to the wife of the King of Israel. Positive, timely and wise influence.

Just like pastors Brian and Bobby Houston and these few Bible women (there are many more) in our spheres of influence, you and I can directly impact our world. At times we may be positive like Esther, mobilising forces for good, sometimes, intercepting problems like Abigail, and at other times negatively affecting others when we are being self-centred and controlling.

I believe most of us desire more than anything to affect change in others in a wonderful way that will last, so keep reading to find ways to do that well.

travelling together

But in the meantime, life is complicated and today's woman is often hard on herself to succeed in a multitude of roles, putting considerable strain on her ability to impact well. Most don't believe they have what it takes to affect others positively, so immersed and overwhelmed are they in their daily treadmill of marriage, children, finances, health and work.

Here are some of the daily issues we women face:

- **Caring for families** – women are generally the carers for both the children and older family members;
- **Hormones** – when some of us might be a nightmare to live with;
- **Being busy** – filling many roles with limited time to fulfil them;
- **Multi-focused** – juggling home, work and the whole world. Today's young women have more to negotiate than their mothers did at the same age.

As a result, our ripples may not extend in good ways due to a lack of fresh flowing input and time from our Maker.

This book has been written to help you discover what you need to become a world changer and a beautiful influence in the process.

We will journey together, trekking into what may seem uncertain territory. At times the expedition will probably feel unfamiliar and foreign. But I assure you the destination is magnificent. It's a place where others in your world are impacted by the woman you are meant to be. God-created and God-breathed, for a unique purpose. It may seem a million miles away right now. But will you trust me, take the plunge and begin?

In the pages of this book we will travel on three journeys across three sections. Together, we'll move from crazy, stressed and frazzled lives to God-inspired peace in the first. In the second, we will dislodge some heavy, emotional baggage, to relocate to a place of un-frazzled freedom. And then lastly in the final section, we'll navigate from negative self-image or low self-esteem to confidence, purpose and a dazzling new you!

1. **Un-frazzled peace** – finding, accessing and remaining in God's peace whilst living in a crazy world;

2. **Un-frazzled freedom** – discovering and dealing with emotional baggage that creates personal and relational tension;

3. **Dazzling influence** – uncovering divine inner beauty and strength to outwardly shine the love of God. What's not to like about those destinations?

Near the end of each chapter I will tell a real-life *before and after* account, describing a difficulty or challenge that women I have personally known faced and overcame as they used the tools described in that chapter.

Following *before and after* will be a summary of the chapter main points called *short and sweet* with some further Bible verses to develop your spiritual walk; then journaling suggestions in *journey journaling* followed by a *prayer* to uplift your spirit.

Like me, do you desire to touch lives wherever we are placed with whatever is in our hand to use? With unique gifts, talents, smiles, friendliness, love, money, time? For me, I'm pouring out to you ripples of encouragement in my words as I tap on my keyboard in 43 degree heat with perspiration trickling down my nose. Giving it away to the best of my ability.

I pray that this book will help you gently dig deep within, to unearth the you that God intended.

Open it at any section or chapter to get strategies for your situation if you are in the midst of a crisis needing immediate solutions. But if you prefer systematic reading, you can start from the beginning, processing each section step by step.

So girl, fasten your seat belt. Get ready to move with me, however you choose to take the reading trip. Prepare to invest and then see the change. It will seep into your spirit and deep into your soul, transforming you from the inside out for incredible influence.

a prayer

Father, help me to be the fantastic influence you have designed by Your supernatural power inside me.

Give me the courage to change and grow surrounded by the safety of Your loving arms of grace and mercy.

Amen.

peta soorkia

SECTION 1

Un-frazZled peace

And the peace of God, which transcends all understanding, will guard your hearts and your minds in Christ Jesus.[1]

... My peace I give to you ...[2]

Influence begins from and operates out of the inner heart. In other words, what's going on inside you affects the world around you. If you are stressed to the max, your impact on others may be less than positive. The reverse is also true. God-delivered inner calm produces outward serenity that can shape the environment and impact a world.

I hope that the reason you are reading this is that you are ready for serenity. If you and I change a little piece of the world and then that starts a ripple, just imagine the effect?

To start the ball rolling, this section will talk about those areas of life that cause stress to you and therefore less than perfect influence. It may reveal a few home truths that you had not previously considered and perhaps be a wake-up call to make some changes. If you choose to do that, at the end of this section you will have strategies and tools to find the peace you long for, enabling you to extend life-giving ripples to your world, beginning a huge ripple effect.

You may think to yourself (as I hear many say to me), "I'm not stressed, just busy."

Before you make that assumption, please read this chapter. I will examine the relationship between your stress, your peace and the cost. Then in the next chapter I will talk about busyness, which I'm pretty sure you can relate to. (Can't we all?) And then finally the de-stress tactics to show you a peace that you can't believe. Let's begin the journey.

Stress, the peace stealer

interruptions to order

A woman's responsibilities – family to care for, daily domestics, full or part-time work. With everything, there is some sort of order to follow. For me, in the past, I felt the need for order most of the time. And when things went wrong, my order was lost. Here's a sample day in the life of Mrs On-The-Go!

Life was full with work, study and writing. On the home front, our house was bursting at the seams with our son back from a year's overseas exchange. Our Ecuadorian homestay girl was around the house on uni break, a new 15-year-old Chinese homestay arriving and our daughter due any day (on holiday from teaching in Alice Springs). I had much to organise on the day in question, so I planned to get my gym and swim dealt with early. Things seemed to be humming along nicely but as we know that may be a sign that disaster is about to strike at any moment. It did in the form of one 17-year-old lunatic cat.

Did I really understand all those years ago when my daughter adopted her, that somehow I would inherit said cat? No, I didn't think that through. Kids grow up and leave and old cats are too fragile to be moved, particularly to a place in the hot centre of Australia. So muggins mum (me), instead of being a distant cat-grandmother with few responsibilities, was now the cat's surrogate mother with all the responsibility. (Beware mums and dads and consider carefully those animals your adoring children are begging for, as kids depart but those furry little creatures may remain.)

Back to the day in question. If you have owned a cat, you probably know that they don't like to be messed with. This elderly feline had been diagnosed with some conditions requiring medication and was strongly rejecting the process of being turned upside down to have cream smeared on her sensitive parts. (I don't think I'd fancy that myself!) And then the process of having her head held back, jaw stretched open for a foreign object (tablet) to be shoved down her throat was also distasteful to the queen of the house. The tail language (whoosh, whoosh) was clearly saying: "Don't do this. I'm warming up to hiss, scratch, maybe even bite you to show who's really in charge, then disappear forever to make you feel guilty ... until the next mealtime ..."

On this morning, tablet hopefully down, she finally escaped to charge around the house, at speeds any self-respecting elderly cat shouldn't attempt! As I endeavoured to leave the house, she began throwing up and doing other unfortunate odourous liquefied deposits right in my pathway at the back door. What a terrible waste of good tuna. Much as I would have loved to ignore these regurgitated and explosive heaps at my feet, in my new role of cat-nanna, I am unfortunately now chief sick and poo-cleaner. Once upon a time, this start to my day would have made me stressed-to-the-max for some time afterwards.

You may not have an elderly cat but we all have moments when stinky messes impede our progress. Unexpected interruptions with the potential to upset us if we allow it. Messy incidents to foil our best-laid plans.

Thankfully, God has taught me (eventually I listened) to rest in Him along the journey of life. Now, cats, people, circumstances, messes happen in my life and I have better strategies to work through them in a calm manner because I'm being recharged regularly as I rest in God's peace. It's a peace that is better than anything[3] and overrides me, my thoughts and the way that I do things. The great thing is that with a little bit of determined effort, it's absolutely free.

choose peace

I've been stressed and busy for as long as I have memories. And at times like these I've found it's easy to forget important things. Like, when my kids were little, dropping them off at school and childcare on the way to work. One time, I got a shock when my eldest daughter spoke to me as I drove into the car park at work. Whoops!! Wasn't she supposed to be at school? Did I forget her? Oh no, another 40 minutes added to an already maxed out day!

Have you found yourself in situations like this? Life so busy, with your head full of anything and everything to be done, with not enough time to do them? If you have young children at home or at school, you will know the stress of organising home and family. You may have teenagers or young adults that you're trying to live with. You may volunteer or look after your grandchildren, or work long hours. You may be studying and working and managing a busy social life. Whatever season you are in, there's plenty to do and therefore plenty to stress about. You may long for some peace but it seems like a pipe dream and impossible to achieve.

If we learn how to regularly rest in God's peace, we can be equipped better to deal with cat poo, baggage or forgetfulness or any other problems that come our way. But even better, some problems or mistakes like these don't even occur in the first place when we can think clearly, rationally and logically.

Sound like dreamworld? And I don't mean the theme park in sunny Queensland. Do you wish you had a life where you could think and strategise? The key is to locate peace in the midst of life's stresses.

peace and stress

All this talk about stress, so what is it? The Oxford Dictionary defines it as: "A state of mental or emotional strain or tension resulting from adverse or very demanding circumstances."[4]

This sounds extreme, but in reality everybody is dealing with and managing a certain amount of stress in the 21st century. How we individually handle it varies widely. If it's ongoing, well-being is compromised as stress and well-being tend to be opposites on a continuum. More of one, less of the other. If you are high on the stress end, you could tend to be low on the peace end.

Should we assume therefore that stress is inevitable in this day and age? I believe not. We can change how we react to the challenging seasons of our lives, if we can be immersed in an inner calm, so deep, that it can cancel out inner and outer pressures to bring about lasting change from the very core of our being. Inner calm...want some?

This is possible and doable for each of us, even me – your classic type-A personality. So don't lose hope for your own situation. But first I want to examine some hard facts about stress and a lack of peace. And exactly what happens if stress is left unchecked. We also need to look at how stress originates. This information I hope may encourage you to make significant but nevertheless achievable changes to how you've been living life.

Most of us generally assume that stress is caused by external circumstances beyond our control. Things such as the weather, natural disasters, the economy or closer to home, people, work, finances, health, ministry and work-life balance. To an extent this is true as our western lifestyle is physically and mentally demanding.

However, although these external things do seem to be the cause of our stress, it's actually what's happening inside of us, or what we feel, or the internal perceptions and emotions, real or imagined about these, that actually produces an internal reaction. These feelings could stem from frustration, anger, anxiety, fear, insecurity, or resentment about those things happening around us. We internalise the external dimensions of our lives. This is the other type of stress, and perhaps the most dangerous because it's largely unseen.

For many of us busyness and other irritations such as time, urgency, impatience, or competitiveness are major factors.[5] We could be worried about the future, feel guilty about the past or feel overwhelmed with the current demands of life. As women, we tend to be more susceptible to stress than men,[6] perhaps because we tend to be juggling home, caring for children and/or aged parents, work and health issues.

What about the younger woman? Stress seems also to be a growing problem for the next generation of women now in their late teens and early 20s. They are reporting more stress than their mothers or grandmothers.[7] I've watched many young women who live with us as international students, immersed in the communication revolution. Computers, iPods, social media, studies, part-time jobs, TV, phones and social activities seem to fill every single moment.

The women I meet at my workshops and those that I coach, tell me the same story. They feel stressed by external pressures causing internal stress. At any given time they could be doing several tasks whilst also thinking about a host of other details. Sound like you?

There are negative consequences to ongoing stress. It's time to stop and take stock. Revisit priorities. Look at the immense costs of stress. To ignore it is like sticking our necks in the sand and ignoring potential long-term problems. To become aware I believe is half the battle won, so now I'm going to begin sharing with you some alarming facts.

Strap yourself in – it might be a rough ride as you learn some truths about how you've been living your life up to now. You might be in for a shock when I start to unpack the range of consequences that stress can cause.

motivators for change

What are the problems you face that cause you unrest or discomfort on a daily basis, or those things that you want to see thrown into the proverbial sea?

> ... whoever says to this mountain, Be lifted up and thrown into the sea! and does not doubt at all in his heart but believes that what he says will take place, it will be done for him.[8]

I shall call these your motivating mountains (MMs) or those things that are your challenges and also your motivators for change. These are those things which if changed or eliminated, would make the most difference to your world.

Read through the following list and select two that are your greatest challenges to your ongoing well-being.

Motivating mountains (MMs) checklist:

- ☐ General stress
- ☐ Health issues
- ☐ Parents
- ☐ Marriage relationship
- ☐ Relationship with kids/teens/extended family
- ☐ Physical demands of young children

- ☐ Boss
- ☐ Work
- ☐ Finances
- ☐ Accommodation/home
- ☐ Anxiety
- ☐ Busyness
- ☐ Needing possessions
- ☐ Pain
- ☐ Emotions
- ☐ Hormonal issues
- ☐ Sleep problems
- ☐ Drained and exhausted
- ☐ Depression
- ☐ Other _____
- ☐ Other _____

In the journey journaling section at the end of this chapter I ask you to journal your top two challenges or motivating mountains whilst imagining how their removal would impact your life. You may want to turn to that section now and note your thoughts.

If you want that then you have what it takes, to work on a new habit of de-stress, instead of the worry-about-anything-and-everything habit that you've previously practised. It's not impossible. It's simply about implementing a new habit.

Many women are now experiencing the unexpected benefits that I did – changes in their reactions to circumstances and stressors. As a result, not just theirs but many lives around them have been significantly changed!

Yours could too, but before I give you some practical strategies in the next two chapters, we first need to take a look at the negative costs of stress on the vessel that is you or me. A tense inner container has the potential to produce waves of turmoil rather than gentle outflows in the pool of life.

stress costs

Several years ago, I was trying to be wonder woman of the year – in my workplace, my home and my neighbourhood. Outwardly oozing success, others saw my achievements and accomplishments in a successful career, a beautiful home, an attentive husband and two beautiful children.

Inwardly, however, this woman wasn't travelling so well. I was trying to measure up, but felt like I was never quite making the grade and that there was always more to do or achieve or learn. I was striving to always improve and win, to satisfy my high goals! I was stressed, frazzled and confused. And it was costing me in more ways than one. I was having issues with sleep, health and my marriage. So how did wannabe wonder woman get this way?

It began when I was 17. After a relationship break-up that ended badly, I was hospitalised in a psychiatric hospital containing people who had given up on life and then a few years later, after a near fatal car accident, I became anxious. Stress began to take a hold of my life. I tried a host of self-help strategies, including meditation, which seemed to temporarily relieve anxiety. In later years and after I became a Christian, I taught fashion design and then communication skills. Included in my subject range was stress management. Me, stressed and anxious, teaching de-stress! My test was about to become my testimony.

God has a way of preparing us for the future. So I researched and became somewhat of an expert in the theory of stress management, whilst simultaneously teaching hundreds of students de-stress progressive body relaxation. This however wasn't enough to save me from what loomed.

God obviously has a sense of humour, calling me to become a staff pastor in my home church. The caring professions are where people's cares become our own, so that the demands of ministry, along with my performance-style character, led to what had been coming my way for some time. Burnout. I lived in a blur on my couch in a state of helplessness for many months, before somehow resuming life once again. I made some changes but nothing significant so there would be more God lessons to learn, a few years on. Burnout reared its ugly head again and it was time to learn some more! About time, right? God had to interrupt my own attempts at dealing with stress for over 20 years whilst trying to fix myself with self-analysis and strategies from the marketplace.

I needed a miracle. And I needed God to come through.

I was ready for anything He suggested – as one day in desperation, close to feeling out of control yet again – I prayed for His divine help. (A good idea for a Bible believing minister right?) I was between a rock and a hard place and I was so desperate with nowhere left to go and nothing else left to try that I actually listened. God wasted no time pointing me to Him and His peace.

I felt God was saying to me to, "rest in Me" during my day. I obeyed (I felt that at this point I had little or no choice, I'd tried the alternatives.) Soon I began to feel healthier than I had for many months, even years. I actually enjoyed a refreshing week's leave rather than a week of recovery. Then, surprise, surprise, I found as time went on and I continued with this new habit of stopping regularly in my day to connect with and rest in God, that I started to react in new and better ways to the normal stressors of life that cause us to come undone. You know these – husband, kids, money, work.

Little did I know of the journey I was about to undertake that would take me from my staff role at church to full-time women's ministry speaking, coaching and writing. God will use our tests to produce wonderful testimonies to help others and glorify Him. In chapter 3 you'll learn about this way of relating to God in meditative peace and silence. This was the beginning of a dramatic change in my life. It was the beginning of real self-care and it has changed everything for me! And it could change everything for you too.

Remember those motivators? Those problems in your life that cause you stress and anxiety? Left unchecked they will cost you dollars and more. So now is a good time to look into what these costs are to wake you a little in the same way that I was woken… although burnout was more than a gentle nudge but a large shove, which I hope you learn quicker than I did!

I am praying that this information might be just what you need to make some decisions to do things differently before you land on your couch or in a psych ward somewhere.

stress and money

Stress costs us money. Millions of dollars apparently. In Australia alone, it's estimated that stress, which often leads to anxiety and depression, costs business and industry nearly $11 billion each year in sick leave and lowered productivity.[9] People spend hard-earned dollars to combat the results of stress by buying books, visiting doctors, sourcing medication and seeing counsellors and therapists.

In my de-stress workshops I ask the participants to total their 'stress' costs for an average month, adding up the costs of things ranging from medical visits, alternative medicines and practitioners to late bill payments and speeding fines, shopping sprees, phone bills, (verbally unloading to our girlfriends can be expensive if your best friend lives in the UK) self-help books, chocolate and coffee 'fixes'. What women tell me they spend is astounding, ranging from hundreds to thousands of dollars every month. What could we women do with that hard cash??

Take a reality check. (See *journey journaling* page 35 for more). Estimate what it costs you to alleviate stress on a monthly basis. See those listed or add your own. Everything from the zone-out movies to the relaxing facials. Your dollar total might surprise or even shock you.

Feeling motivated yet to finding a way to introduce peace and removing some stress from your life? If the hip pocket doesn't convince you, I have more! There are other prices we pay.

Being stressed can affect your decisions.

clear thinking? forget it!

In my early working years (before I was a Christian), I worked in North London for a furniture firm, displaying the company's furniture in retail outlets all over North London. It was an exciting and rewarding job, but also challenging to drive around that large city particularly after dark in the colder months.

I remember vividly one early evening on my way home to the north, travelling along a major motorway that circled London to the north, from east to west. I was trying to find my way to the main northern exit in the dark and with unfamiliar

1 – stress, the peace stealer

village names, I was becoming increasingly concerned that I was travelling in the wrong direction. This is a 26 mile (40 km) long motorway and the more stressed I became, the less I recognised any village names in order to exit. Worry led to increased panic and less rational thinking. I found I was indeed travelling the wrong way as I thought coherently to exit and get directional help. It became a very late night as I finally began again in the right direction. Although it was cold I was sweating with the stress and worry of being lost.

When you are stressed, do you find it a challenge to solve simple routine problems and think logically? Do you tend to be forgetful, leave belongings behind and find it difficult to process your thoughts? Some of these thinking issues could be the result of ongoing, chronic stress.

During high stress, the body sets up a response in preparation for danger. This is known as the flight or fight response, one designed by God for humans to be physically proactive in an emergency. Hormones in our brains send signals to our body to produce energy in our muscles. For this to occur, non-essential areas, such as digestion, the bowel and some areas of the brain slow down, so that the blood flow can be diverted to areas requiring the energy such as the muscles. As a result of the redirected blood flow, brain activity is limited to only carrying out basic survival operations rather than operating any creative or detailed processing. These high capacity areas simply won't operate as there's no blood present. No blood flow to the brain's thinking areas means lessened analytical brain activity.

My internal panic on that day in London caused a physical stress response (sweating and tense muscles) which biologically reduced my ability to think logically. And the reverse is also true as Dr Caroline Leaf, a Christian psychologist tells us. She says our thoughts affect our stress levels which in turn affect thinking, emotions and words in either life-giving or toxic ways.

> "No system of the body is spared when stress is running rampant. A massive body of research collectively shows that up to 80% of physical, emotional and mental health issues today could be a direct result of our thought lives."[10]

Is it any wonder that God is so interested in our thought life?

> And now, dear brothers and sisters, one final thing. Fix your thoughts on what is true, and honourable, and right, and pure, and lovely, and admirable. Think about things that are excellent and worthy of praise.[11]

From our thoughts, let's move to talk more about our emotions. Eek!

the emotional roller coaster

In the early years of my marriage, I used to lie awake in the middle of the night crying about my relationship with my husband. I felt emotionally alone as our communication was less than I had hoped for. During those long nights, I couldn't seem to escape my emotions. I was governed by them, ruled by them and didn't have a clue that I could change my thinking, instead believing that my circumstances were dictating how I felt.

Now I don't mean to minimise any awful circumstances that you might find yourself in and the understandable effect on how you feel in your marriage or other difficult circumstances you may face. There are some events and people that do cause distress (such as abuse) and these do need to be addressed before major emotional changes can occur. But for many of us, and for me in particular, the normal ups and downs of life take on bigger-than-life proportions if we let them take over our thinking. One reason

1 – stress, the peace stealer

for crazy emotions is hormones.

Emotions are particularly crazy for some females when our hormones are doing backflips during PMS (pre-menstrual syndrome) around the time of the proverbial 'month'. These hormonal changes can cause our emotions to be triggered. And for those of us a little more mature, menopausal symptoms mean the hormones go off the planet too, which can trigger the same sorts of ups and downs emotionally. I used to tell people that my 14-year peri-menopausal season was like experiencing PMS 24/7. Not fun ... for me, or anyone else in my world. I blamed everyone and everything for how I felt, but mostly I blamed my husband. I was supersensitive and touchy about the smallest of things and expected others to fix themselves to make things better for me. I was slightly crazy at times. After all, 'When Mama ain't happy, ain't no-one happy'! And in this case those nearest and dearest knew they'd better run for cover!

You may or may not relate to emotional effects of hormonal change, but if you're female, you can probably relate to emotional highs and lows. Do you worry, get angry, or anxious or when upset, do you cry, shout, withdraw, panic or lose sleep? Have you felt at times like you are losing it or have lost it completely and seem irrational? These emotions and the reasons for them seem very real at the time but if not checked over time, they can lead to more difficult and wide-ranging psychological problems such as depression, bipolar or anxiety.[12] Women suffer from these emotional issues to almost twice the extent of men[13] and this is pretty much constant across western cultures. As women we were created with a range of emotions to help our families be nurtured with care and compassion, but God also has answers to our thought life and emotions if we care to implement them.

Since learning to cap my emotional thought life (see

section 2) and drawing in God's peace, I don't stay up in the middle of the night crying about my life any more. I prefer to sleep. If I do get up to cry, it's to pray for others who are hurting and my tears are for their pain as I hand them over to God. It's a much better way to go about things, surrendering them to God if I must be up at all. I like my beauty sleep which I definitely need as I get older. So (on the inside) letting go and letting God do His stuff helps me to react in more positive ways to life. And this has had a significant and positive impact on my relationship with my husband. (Thank goodness, he says! Me too!)

So with that example, let's look further into the cost of stress on our relationships. If we are doing OK and getting along well with people, then the rest of our life seems to flow beautifully. But unfortunately, this is not always the case.

getting along

The intersection of people and viewpoints can cause problems and stress to those involved. And outside stresses can also be affected by bearing the brunt. What results can be misunderstandings, conflict, unforgiveness, blame, bitterness, envy, isolation, inability to trust, or a host of other issues further increasing stress. Eventually separation, loneliness, heartache and divorce can be the heartbreaking results.

Many relationships break down not because of large problems but because of many small ones that add up over time. One newly-wed wife and friend of mine was terribly upset with how the marriage wasn't living up to what she had expected so that little things were becoming major for her. One day when her husband cut his toenails whilst she was sweeping the floor, she was ready to give up on the marriage. Little issues build into large ones.

What about gender differences? Men and women respond to stress differently.

Women react differently to men during stress after the initial fight/flight response. Women will tend to reach out to others for support which increases the feel-good hormones (progesterone and oxytocin).

Men have their own stress response, producing testosterone which can increase aggression and competition.[14] Perhaps God created this for emergency situations as we girls cluck around all care and share. In God's design, I see this as a good balance of responsibilities and responses. However, in today's culture, the balance between men's and women's roles is more blurred and uncertain, causing stress about the way each should respond. No wonder we don't understand each other! The women are clucking and the guys (with extra doses of testosterone) are shouting.

Jesus identified the age-old human condition called sin as requiring us to examine ourselves before pointing out others' (or our spouse's) faults. At stressful times, it is difficult, if not impossible, to think clearly about our own or others' actions. Small issues tend to look bigger when under this type of pressure. If we can first look inward, this can go a long way to paving the way for understanding.

That's what happened to me as I learned a new way to relax in the middle of a relational 'situation' with my husband. Instead of the normal quick retort when upset, I learned to zip the lip, walk away and connect with God for a few minutes. His grace rubbed off on me so that I began to change how I reacted to conflict within our marriage. Such a small strategy but effective and influential. And hubby's testosterone didn't skyrocket so he began to react differently, more gently, towards me.

In reality, though, none of us is perfect. We all muck up, make mistakes even though we're all trying to do our best to live life well and in harmony with others. In the midst of relational strife and if we want to do things God's way, His grace shown to us can go a long way through our own hearts as we extend this same grace to others.

One of the most dangerous results of stress is the next area – our health. There is a significant physical cost to our bodies of ongoing stress.

stress costs health

Ageing is a natural part of living and it's hard when we notice the grey hairs and wrinkles appearing. Ouch! Reality check, time is marching on and we are too.

A certain recipe for physical problems and even more wrinkles is a hyped-up, turbo-charged body. The fight or flight response, as previously explained, prepares us to be ready for attack or for an emergency situation with high levels of adrenalin and cortisol produced for emergency situations, but not for everyday living. When the stress hormones are raging the feel-good hormones that produce relational warmth, peace and affection towards others tend to be suppressed, compromising the immune system and causing slower physical healing and recovery.[15]

Living like this causes too much of a load on the body's functions.

As a result the body becomes more susceptible to illness and physiological symptoms. These include blood rushing to the head, a pounding heart, tight muscles, headaches, high blood pressure, IBS (irritable bowel syndrome) or other chronic health issues. Our body in fight or flight mode makes the lungs work harder and the heart beat faster, raising blood pressure. The skin sweats; fats, sugars and cholesterol in the bloodstream increase; the stomach secretes more acid; the immune system slows and blood vessels constrict.[16] These are signs that stress is disturbing God's perfect design for the body's operation and living well into old age.

Living stressed is similar to driving a car, with one foot on the accelerator and the other on the brake! We're using up petrol (bodily functions) but not expending the required energy. This means that the body organs are working harder than they need to and wearing out early. A disturbing factor now emerging from medical research is that chronic stress that produces high levels of cortisol and adrenaline can take six to nine months to reduce to manageable levels![17] It will take more than a cuppa and a good sleep to reduce those raging hormones.

But it's not all doom and gloom. You've come to the right place (reading this book) so hang with me a little longer. But the hard facts need to be told and after all, I know what constant stress feels like. I've been there and I'm here to tell you the flip side of the story. I pray and hope that my journey and the stories of others will save you the same struggle in your search for freedom from strife to become the life-giving vessels God desires.

The next two chapters will give you practical strategies in order for you too to achieve this.

before and after

Kim, a young married executive had been head-hunted from the UK to work in a high-powered, male-dominated industrial role in Australia. Long days, hour after hour of meetings day after day, plus high levels of responsibility were taking their toll on her health, well-being and as a consequence the rest of her life.

I met her just after she had been diagnosed with painful IBS (irritable bowel syndrome) and endometriosis, causing potential infertility. These painful health issues were impacting her in many ways so that now both her work and social activities were being affected. All medical help had been investigated and as a last resort Kim decided to examine whether stress was a contributing factor in her ill health. We all live with stress but for many of us it is difficult to accept that our actions are causing negative consequences and that these may require habit and lifestyle changes. After exhausting her search for medical interventions with little or no improvement, Kim arrived at a place of surrender to God, looking for a new way to live.

Initially, it was difficult to get to this place mentally. Kim had been an ordered and full-on, work-smart woman for her entire working life. But pain can be a great motivator. So she made some decisions, reassessed her priorities and took action to implement de-stress strategies. She recognised that not eating lunch or taking breaks during her day, coupled with busy after hours church and social schedules, needed to be addressed. She began by taking regular time out during the day and attending to her thoughts and emotions. There was very little change for many months, but she persevered with encouragement to not give up and happily, towards the end of 12 months, things began to turn around.

A medical operation at this time showed that the endometriosis had miraculously begun to reduce and she felt that the IBS symptoms were also slowly beginning to lessen for the first time in many years.

Kim was moved by negative health issues. They seemed insurmountable mountains of ill health and pain. These dark places make us take stock of the cost of ongoing stress caused by overwork. Kim as a result became open to what God was doing and changed her ways, and learned the hard lessons. She put in place much needed margins, relaxing strategies and then finally persevered. A new Kim emerged with better and healthier outcomes for her future.

short and sweet

- Women have responsibilities and are busy in the mix. Interruptions may mean that order is lost, which can be upsetting. This is an invitation for God to step in if we'll let Him.
- Stress can cause strain and other symptoms that are uncomfortable to live with.
- Stress and peace don't co-exist, John 14:27.
- Stress is how we respond to outside events in our lives, Matt. 6:25; Phil. 4:6.
- Stress and busyness do not have to be the norm for the rest of your life, Rom. 12:2.
- Busyness and other irritations are major factors in causing stress.
- Ongoing stress can lead to chronic stress, burnout, and negative influence. Luke 10:41, 12:22-29; Phil. 4:6.
- God will allow us to get to a tough place in order for us to rest in Him and begin real self-care which has the power to change everything.
- Stress costs us in money terms; clear thinking, rational thinking, emotionally and physically, Luke 12:22-32;
- Stress also costs us in our relationships with others, Mark 14:50.
- Solving simple routine problems and thinking logically is difficult under stress. This is because the body prepares for an emergency, sending energy to the muscles.
- Many women suffer anxiety, but God has a plan for us to deal with stress if we would slow down, Ps. 46:10.
- A hyped-up body causes a load on the body's

functions which affects bodily function and is similar to carrying heavy baggage on our shoulders, Phil. 4:6.
- Prolonged stress compromises the immune system and causes slower healing and recovery times.
- Chronically high levels of stress hormones can take six months to reduce.
- Any new habit takes a decision, perseverance, time and practise. Phil. 4:13.

journey journaling

Write down your thoughts:

- What are the problems (MMs) you face that cause you unrest or discomfort? Can you see how they could be motivation for change? If so journal your thoughts.
- What impact would the removal of these mountains have on your well-being?
- Take a reality check and estimate stress and its cost to you financially, on a monthly basis. Consider these costs below and others that you may think about.
    - facials
    - movies to zone out
    - self-help books
    - doctors
    - medication
    - counsellors
    - alternative therapists
    - alternative medicine

- late bill payments
- speeding fines
- shopping sprees
- phone bills
- chocolate and coffee fixes

- Write down, under the following headings, other costs in these areas:
  - clear thinking
  - emotions
  - relationships
  - physical health and well-being
  - productivity
- Check out the following scriptures and note one or two that give you a sense of peace right now in your present circumstances.
- Ps. 29:11; Isa. 26:3; Jer. 29:11-12; Mat. 6:33; Phil. 4:7; Eph. 2:14; 2 Thes. 3:16.

a prayer

> Lord, I ask you to reveal those areas in my life where stress is costing me. Open my eyes to see and then my heart to respond to Your leading. Help me to make the tough decisions to prioritise how I do things. I need Your help and Your strength as I trust You on this journey of growth. Thank You in Jesus' name. Amen.

2

Getting off the treadmill

In the previous chapter we investigated how stress steals our peace and how much that ongoing stress costs us not just financially but in a range of ways that can seriously affect our life and well-being. In this chapter we will navigate and unpack the importance of self care in the midst of time-poor busy lives. Then the final chapter in this section will show you how to apply the Bible to de-stress in the midst of stress and busyness.

self care

Caring for ourselves seems common sense, but it's not easy for us as women. It requires us to put personal self care as a priority ... along with all the other must-do items on our to-do lists. We girls are God's best carers but we're not so good at caring for ourselves. Why is that?

Perhaps it's the carer instinct in our nature, which tends to put other's needs at a higher priority and our needs somewhere down the bottom of the list. Certainly it's more blessed to give than receive[1], but it's hard to give something away when we're so exhausted that there's nothing left to hand out. In this day and age and in my experience with the women I meet at conferences and in my coaching practice, we are abysmally poor at taking time out. Instead, we push through whilst surviving on less than adequate rest.

So why don't we stop what we're doing to take a break? Mistakenly, most of us figure that we'll finish a task then stop. If that's you, then join the club! But you know as well as I do that more jobs keep appearing, so that we don't stop as we ignore the tell-tale signs of tiredness. We begin to think that tiredness, even exhaustion, is the norm for our lives.

It's a sobering fact that even if you and I did all the home and work tasks that beckon, there still wouldn't be enough hours in the day. Unfortunately, this type of living may lead to chronic stress and cause other related problems over time as we saw in chapter 1.

Now what about time (or lack of) and the constant busyness of life? Do these press your buttons like they do mine? What exactly are we so busy about and how do you and I slow down to have the time and energy to do what we are meant to?

busy isn't best

I guess you could call me a high achiever. I love to cross items off my to-do list and I get lots of things completed in this way. A Christian pastor friend that I worked with on church staff for years always joked that he would like to bottle my blood, in order to achieve what I did. But I persevere even when it's to my harm. And in fact, I think I've been wearing my busyness a bit like a badge of honour. It sounds so important to be doing this, going here, meeting with so-and-so. It's pride. And it's ugly. As well as doing me harm. Filling every available moment. For what purpose, I wonder? Are we impressing anyone or just running ourselves into an early grave?

Are you like this? I've been noticing many others who are. In the checkout lane, we meet a friend or acquaintance and ask how they are. The answer is often, 'oh I'm busy, you know'. Working women, stay-at-home women, retired women, all women seem to be busy doing. Everybody engaged in important doing-ness. And does this make us more wanted, or needed?

It might look very admirable to those who tend to procrastinate or have difficulty achieving the dreams they have for their lives, but this achieving style has its downside as I found to my detriment during and after the ravages of burnout! When my couch seemed to me to be the only place of safety because praying, thinking, relating became almost impossible, I began to realise that busy is certainly not best.

Stopping and taking good quality time out just for the sake of it is God inspired. God designed rest so it must be a pretty good idea. It's also essential for good health and living life well. Rest plus God is an awesome twosome, producing multiplied benefits.

It's okay to not always be achieving and doing, doing, doing 24/7! It's fine to slow down or stop. Do you need to slow down the pace and flow a little slower doing things a different way? God's way? If you let Him, He will carry you His way.

> For each day he carries us in his arms.[2]

perfect timing

> For everything there is a season, a time for every activity under heaven.[3]

Do you ever feel that you're so busy worrying about tomorrow or feeling bad about yesterday that somehow today got lost? For many of us, we are consumed with what happened yesterday or might happen in the future. For some this causes procrastination, the fear of failure triggering immobilisation. What a terrible way to live. But how often do we spend our now, thinking about another time? I have lived most of my life like this. I'm learning that in reality, the present is the only time zone in which we actually exist, and the saying, *there's no time like the present*, rings true. It will be too soon that our lives are over.

> ... You sweep people away like dreams that disappear. They are like grass that springs up in the morning. In the morning it blooms and flourishes, but by

evening it is dry and withered.[4]

In fact, our here and now is actually what life is all about. Yesterday has gone and tomorrow hasn't arrived. By not excessively dwelling on the past and future, we are able to focus and pay attention to the only liveable time, here and now.

Being truly present, enjoying the people and experiences that are on offer somehow seems to stretch out our now time, strange as this sounds. I have found personally that my nows feel fuller, more expanded and richer as I focus on this moment and what is going on in me and around me. In Hebrews 3:7, we are told *today, listen to His voice...* (paraphrased). God has something on offer today. In your *now*. Don't miss it.

> *This is the day the Lord has made. We will rejoice and be glad in it.*[5]

Our moments in life pass too quickly. Now in my 50s with grown children, (grandchildren nowhere in sight, get a move on kids please), it only seems like yesterday that I birthed my children (the natural but excruciatingly hard way – I'm sure you remember if you are a mother. If not, you'll thank me one day. I'm preparing you). It seems as if it was only another moment before they were off to school and then a breath away, later to university.

I remember these memorable events as if they were recent, rather than more than 20 years ago. In a flash they are, then they are not, never to return. Instead of hurrying through or getting stuck within the mundane and tediousness of the present, I wish that I had enjoyed those wonderful times as they were happening.

Our *now* time is too important an event to miss because our brains are elsewhere. We can enjoy more peace and fun as a series of small or large significant now moments expand and join to become an overall satisfying life.

To enjoy now, look around. Who is in your world? Can you release some of His overflow? Give them a hug or offer a word of encouragement. What else do you see? Look for God's awesome creation. Now look in the mirror. Who is there? You, God's precious girl. And you are here now in the place you are at, God ordained for such a time as this, (see Esther 4:14).

Be in your here and in your now. Why not get started straight away?

Let me also say here that there is much benefit to be had from examining and learning from our past experiences. We can be freed up from any excess emotional baggage that we have unknowingly loaded onto our shoulders, (see section 2 for more on being freed from the past).

And it's also a good idea to think about and prepare for (rather than worry about) the future, in order to look forward to the promising tomorrows that God has planned for us.

> ... I know the thoughts and plans that I have for you, says the Lord, thoughts and plans for welfare and peace and not for evil, to give you hope in your final outcome.[6]

planning tomorrows

Your *tomorrows* are the result of your planning *today*. If we expect our future to be different without doing anything different, we'll be disappointed. Great tomorrows mean planning, thinking and organising those pizza nights with friends, or picnics in the park. Or that study you've always dreamed about doing. We have to act. God is depending on you and me to do what He has called us to do on the Earth. Wonderful and amazing only-you-can-do things.

2 – getting off the treadmill

So how do we plan? Many women I work with are stuck and can't move forward in any direction because they don't know in what direction to move. The key is knowing God's plan for our lives.

We need a clear head to hear Him which requires putting time aside to listen. Getting rid of stress generally helps women to hear God and this is covered in detail in chapter 3. Once you practise finding His peace and His voice is being heard again or for the first time, it's a wonderful and beautiful time to prayerfully ask God for His agenda for your life. From here, plans can be made and strategic actions can begin.

I suggest you block out time to find out your God-given direction. An hour or more without distractions (notify others) can give you a sense of what He wants for you, so you can head in the general direction. This will help give you purpose and perseverance when things get tough with a million distractions.

This is you spending some of your now time on your future. Believing God will do it through you will achieve a great future for you, your purpose and your family.

If you have heard from God or something deep within you cries to be done by you, go and do some research, thinking about the logistics. In other words, what needs to happen and when? There is a bit to consider when thinking about tomorrow.

It's good to then write down what you want to achieve, making these your goals. Putting pen to paper gets your dreams into a more real format and gives you a focus. Once you have your goals then break them into small chunks to create a SMART plan such as:

- S is for specific so write down under each main goal, small and doable steps that lead to the larger goal;
- M is for measurable which means write the date or times when it will be achieved and also how much will be achieved in precise numbers;
- A is for achievable. Check that each small step plus the major goals are achievable in this season of your life;
- R is for relevant and what is right for you with your strengths and limitations;
- T is for time-framed. Organise the timing for each step progressively to reach the date of your desired goal outcome.

In my work with women we set up goal indicators to measure the change on the journey. I suggest that for you now, in order to keep you on track. Perhaps have someone to be accountable to in order to help you stay focussed. Monthly you can ask yourself (or be asked) how you are going on a scale from 1-10, what worked and what didn't work and what can you do to move one notch up the scale for the next month.

Put these few small strategies in place and who knows? The world may just become a better place because of what you and only you can achieve! Pray for it, believe it, and you'll see it.

Faith is the confidence that what we hope for will actually happen; it gives us assurance about things we cannot see.[7]

a *personal recharge*

Some days, it seemed like I'd got out of the wrong side of the bed. Too much to do and never-ending pressure. Like a well-worn car, my body needs a service occasionally to get

2 – getting off the treadmill

all the parts working again. Like a car, a body needs some time off the road for a grease and oil change (or a movie and popcorn or a good book). Overtired or overused, the emotions invariably got the better of me, so that I eventually lost the plot and got cranky. Not pretty. Tears, pouting, sullen silences. Yuk. My poor husband would roll his eyes and I would know that I'd gone too far. I'd be upset with others, because I felt my load was their fault. No. Often it was not. It was my inability to say no and therefore doing too much.

How to then recharge our bodies and inner spirit and soul in the 21st century when we seem to be busy about being busy? Particularly when we have families, work, church and a myriad of priorities? My experience working with hundreds of women tells me that, often, time to recharge has been forgotten or pushed to the side of our never-ending to-do list.

Somehow, you and I need to rest by taking some well-earned breaks. Our body requires us to do this or over time, as we discussed in the previous chapter, there could be serious costs to our health and well-being. We need ways to build health-giving breaks into our lives in order to allow our bodies to recuperate. It may begin with inserting some boundaries, building margins into our schedule and finding ways to laugh out loud. May I suggest to you (and to myself) that these important but seemingly not-so-urgent ways to achieve downtime, are in fact more necessary than anything else on your to-do list.

If we as women don't rest up, our lives of doing, doing and never done, will in fact, do us! Do us to death that is. We need to slow down as well as learn to say no! We'll look at both of these boundary forming habits now.

stop doing

Always moving, never-ending activity. No time to stop. If that's you, then you will need to find some discipline to change. Some people may need others to come along and gently and lovingly boot them into reality to make those changes. You may need reminding of your worth instead of always doing for others whilst you run ragged on the inside.

Do you believe that it's difficult, or impossible, for you to get off your busy treadmill? Most women I talk to know that they should slow down, but don't know how to. Like them, you probably know that the occasional break will improve your well-being producing beneficial flow-on effects to those you love and care for.

Finding rest, and as a result peace, starts with the recognition that you need a break to stop the cycle of constant activity. I tell myself that stopping for a few minutes will not cause a world war or a mass strike. Being super-stressed makes mama see things as ten times worse anyway. I continue talking to myself, by saying that walking away from a task for a few minutes will mean that I face it more optimistically on my return. Try talking sensibly to yourself. (My mother loves to joke that talking to oneself is reasonable because we are the only sensible one listening anyway!)

The fact is that others won't notice yours or my short break, but they'll definitely notice if we lose the plot. In the meantime, those dishes won't go anywhere (unfortunately) but will not look quite so daunting after a short, personal reviving interval. Even the laundry floor covered with the daunting task of a week's dirty clothes may look reasonable on returning from a restful God-inspired breather. By the way, God does do miracles. Someone else might even get in there and get the job done. Hallelujahs all round!

Once we have learnt to manage those never-ending tasks around us, the next step is to learn to decisively say no (when necessary) to others, particularly when the requests fall outside our acceptable boundaries. No is such a small word and should be easy to say out loud. Should be, but isn't for many women who find it impossible to say it.

say no! Oh no!

Saying 'no' to others! From your very own lips. Shock, horror! Yes, that's right. A big fat no!

Get ready to say it now. Let's practise out loud, with me.

Nnnn…oooo…oooo.

There you are. It wasn't too bad was it? Get used to it. It's one of the smallest yet powerful words in the English language.

Saying no lovingly to others is in reality setting a boundary. Perhaps difficult but necessary to prevent us doing things that aren't ours to do. It stops us running around chasing our tails, resenting other people when in fact it was our choice to say yes or no and we chose yes. It's a useful word with people who knowingly or unknowingly try to control us to do, say or think things that we would rather not.[8] Healthy boundaries might be difficult to initially put in place but in the end they are better for us than being passive and putting up with things that are sinful or even harmful to our well-being.

God talks about burdens and loads. God says burdens should be co-carried to help others. But he also talks about when we should say no to others' loads, as a load is meant to be a person's individual responsibility to carry, as compared to the sharing of burdens.

Bear one another's burdens, and so fulfil the law of

*Christ ... For each one shall bear his own load.*⁹

We are at times responsible to assist others with their burdens. This word burden here in the Greek means excess burdens too heavy for one and weighing us down. In difficult times of tragedy and pain we need others and they need us. But at other times, we are to carry our personal load, which in the Greek means our daily cargo and toil. It is doable for one. We are meant therefore, to carry our own feelings, attitudes and responsibilities that God has entrusted to us.¹⁰

What this means is that for each of us, it's really important to know what the boundary or cut off point is, of our responsibility versus the responsibilities of other people. To our responsibilities we should say yes and to what is not ours we should say no. It's where we put a line in the sand or shut the gate to our world, letting good in and bad out. God limits His world or house, saying no to sin and invites people (a yes) to those who will believe in and love Him.¹¹ They're His boundaries. What are yours?

If you have children, there comes a point in their development when they must take ownership of things like money, keeping their room tidy and helping with household chores. If parents continue to do these then they are not training the child to stand on their own feet and live as adults. Loving too much can be detrimental to that child as an adult. Saying no to your kids is setting healthy boundaries. Allowing natural consequences is a part of this process. In other words, no pocket money or trips to the movies without chores completed. Allowing benefits without consequences for boundaries teaches irresponsibility.

Loving parents who have family members struggling with addictions, or who control or abuse, need to say no to these behaviours for the future good of all. For the offender to reap the consequences of their behaviour is in their

2 – getting off the treadmill

long-term interest! I once heard of a drug-addicted young woman who had taken money and items from the family home to sell to buy drugs and when her parents stopped supplying money and began hiding their precious household items, she appealed to the grandparents. Out of their misguided love they continued to fund her habit, giving her money. Her parents' tough love is more likely to bring about change in inappropriate behaviour, even though it is often initially more difficult.

Saying no is sometimes the best thing you can do. It may be tough particularly if you have allowed things for a time. It may require strong support from others to help when the going gets tough. But with time, things do improve if you stick to your guns. Think carefully before you act. Practise saying something like, *"I would love to do what you are asking, but unfortunately I can't because ..."* Or how about a loving, *"no, sorry, I can't do that at this time."* Or even a simple *"no, sorry!"* You might like to have some mentor or coach support in place, consider what it will look like. (Sometimes, saying no to others when you've said yes in the past brings on WWIII, so get prepared to stand your ground, then go for no).

I remember a time having lunch with a relative outside of my immediate family that required me to lovingly say no to some unwanted and unnecessary behaviour on their part. A wonderful mentor friend was encouraging me by text, giving me the courage to do the difficult task with love and gentleness.

However you get the job done, setting strong boundaries might just mean that you finally get to do those things that you've always dreamed of, like study, dance classes, picnics on the beach or simply reading a good book with your feet up. Being busy might make us look important to others, but it has negative consequences in the long term.

what stop looks like

The word stop may mean a variety of things to different people. It could mean resting, lying on a sunny beach (yes, that's for me) or on a bed, (that sounds pretty good too). Or it could mean engaging in recreational fun like playing sport (nope). But do these things allow the body to recover and recuperate?

how do you define rest?

Most people take time out from their working lives in order to supposedly rest, but often this is to do something. It might be to take a walk, go to the park, hang out with friends, play a game with the kids or watch a movie. Perhaps you may enjoy siting at your computer or on your phone on Facebook or other social media with time flying and enjoyment levels high. Engaging in these or other enjoyable activities where time seems to stand still produce flow which can be beneficial for our mental health.[12] Although therapeutic, such recreational activities are not enough to allow for the body organs to recover to replenish depleted reserves.

Are weekends your rest time? Most women I know fill their precious days with more activities, such as with the kids or catching up on the housework, shopping and laundry. Do you fit in visits to friends and family and some exercise? All important tasks with some associated and beneficial value but these still require physical exertion. In themselves, they don't produce real rest or body recovery!

So is it the holiday on the beach that gives us the recovery time our body needs to recharge? Taking extended holidays and time away from busy work and home schedules is something we all look forward to. (I'm thinking about a sun-drenched beach, freshly squeezed

2 – getting off the treadmill

juices, warmth and gentle waves – my kind of holiday).

But perhaps you have noticed that it takes a while to unwind when you first get away. Sometimes it takes some time. This could be a result of starting out on the holiday with high stress levels and hormones to boot, which can take days or more to even begin to lessen.

Unfortunately, there is still opportunity for high stress levels between those well-earned breaks! And as wonderful and necessary as these extended breaks are to a balanced lifestyle, they don't make up for the rest of the year lived maxed out to the full.

If our bodies are on overdrive and continually wound up, is there a way to achieve real rest? Like a car, not just a full service is needed (the extended yearly holiday). Many shorter, smaller services to keep the car humming along nicely (such as regular body/mind rests) are also essential for our health to hum along. Real recovery is not simply recreation but full body recovery, when organs slow down and mental agility takes a back seat. The body can then fully recover to more 'restful' states and this can occur during sleep and deep restful mind and body rest.

Deep meditative rest has been popular for some years but in reality has been around since biblical times. It's stopping for real peace deep down in our soul which can help to achieve real rest and, like sleep, is significant to well-being and body recovery. Sleep is God's natural way to top up and is essential for health. Most of us can't take periodic naps in our day to give us a quick shot of energy but we can take small meditative breaks (chapter 3).

The key is having a good balance of activities. Meaningful work, recreation, fun, regular daily restful times and sleep will all assist the body to recover from the daily stress of life. Before I give you some achievable ways to regularly rest (chapter 3), we will look at some God-designed ways to rest, such as sleep and laughter.

sweet sleep

We all need sleep. It's the way we are replenished to live another day. With a good night's sleep, we can take on the world. In fact people who sleep on average 7-8 hours each night have potentially better life expectancy than those who regularly receive much less.[13]

However not everyone sleeps well. As many as one in three people struggle in this area[14] and I'm one of them. My mother tells, that to get me to sleep during the first year of my life, she literally dosed me with a full bottle of brandy (not all at once I hasten to add). I guess brandy did in those days what Phenergan does today for a restless, colicky baby. Although the brandy story is humourous, it is often the case with some who have battled sleeplessness from the beginning of life or for some women with the change of life around their mid-50s.

If you have ever suffered with insomnia or reduced sleep, it can be very unpleasant and in some cases debilitating. Missing sleep for only a few days can seriously impair optimum living by causing irritability, fatigue, impaired concentration and memory issues.[15] Know the feeling? This impairment is comparable with extreme amounts of alcohol or drugs in the system.

Sleeplessness might be a problem in today's society as pressures and stresses have increased. In a recent Australian study, anxiety or depression in women was linked with sleep issues,[16] particularly with the younger and older woman. These sleep problems can range from difficulty getting to sleep, waking during sleep and/or waking early unable to return to sleep.[17]

2 – getting off the treadmill

My husband is a wonderful sleeper (bless him). Whenever and wherever he is, he can sleep and sleep well. Many in his family are the same. In my extended family however, many sleep minimal hours, night after night. It could be genetic – early research is pointing to this fact.[18]

But what about you and me? What can we do to get enough rest to live our lives to the fullest? Although each of us requires a different amount of sleep, between six and nine hours is considered normal. Too little and even too much isn't beneficial for our health.

Where possible try to achieve adequate sleep for your needs. If sleeplessness is an issue for you, here are some sleep tips that might improve your chances of a good night's sleep.

- Develop a similar routine for waking and sleeping times, so that your body clock (circadian rhythm), knows when to sleep and when to wake.

- Your night-time routine might include praying, reading something calming, a warm shower or bath, lights on low (helps melatonin production which enhances sleep) or other activities to help you settle.

- Don't go to bed until you are tired, or you may lay awake then get anxious about not sleeping.[19]

- Try to avoid daytime short naps. Although these naps might be a way of regaining your perk, they can interfere with a regular sleep pattern. (Although, Thomas Edison, Winston Churchill and J.F. Kennedy all took naps!).[20]

- Daily exercise might help.

- Reduce or cut out evening stimulants like caffeine or tyrosine (found in cheeses or chocolate), coffee, tea, colas, MSG (monosodium glutamate sometimes found

in Asian cooking) or cigarettes.[21]
- Don't be hungry or over-full at bedtime.
- Limit foods before bed that could cause the digestion to work such as fatty foods like chips or crisps or nuts, raw vegetables, fruits or beans.
- Promote sleep environment, i.e. a good bed, pillow, bedding, dark lighting, low noise levels, comfortable temperature.
- Sort things out before bedtime in your mind or with others. Don't go to bed anxious or angry (Phil. 4:6). Journal and get a God perspective if you need to.
- Try 'boring' yourself to sleep by playing alphabet games, saying poems or verses, listening to a clock or the breathing of your spouse.[22]
- During a restless night, try not to get agitated or stressed. It may help to get up and do something relaxing like meditating, reading or drinking a herbal tea to interrupt anxious thoughts.
- See your doctor for intervention if insomnia is interfering with your daily activities – there are non-drug interventions by medical health professionals.[23]

When it comes down to it, I believe God created sleep so He probably has the best answer. For me, resting in His peace before I sleep and doing a form of meditation such as God Moments as I sleep and when I wake during the night often works for me.

In peace I will both lie down and sleep, for You, Lord, alone make me dwell in safety and confident trust.[24]

Whatever is causing sleeplessness, God has our sleep answers. So for me going to Him in my heart and mind at bedtime works most times to send me into a restful sleep. On other difficult nights I move to another room or bed, open up my Bible and trust that it will work out somehow. I generally finally fall asleep, am sleepy the next day then try again the next night, expectant that this night I'll sleep better and I generally do. Sweet dreams.

Next I want to look at laughter, an easy way to get some free pleasurable feel-good hormones coursing through the body.

laugh out loud

I will discuss happiness in more depth later in Un-frazzled Freedom but for now I have a suggestion for you to unlock some of the wonderful benefits of happiness. It's something that we should all do more of. Kids do it all the time, and we as adults seem to lose it to a degree. Laughter. Pretty funny, huh? But laughter has fantastic health benefits.

Present-day studies into well-being have uncovered that happiness, smiling and laughter protect us from the negative effects of stress. In fact the positive physical and emotional benefits as a result of regularly being happy, with recurring doses of laughter, are staggering. These simple God-given gifts to us produce better health in the short and long-term, increase our life span, and help us to better perform in all areas of life.[25] Amazing stuff that God has already given this information in the Bible from long ago and now modern-day science is backing this up.

The joy of the Lord is my strength.[26]

So why not hang out with some of your funny friends? You might think of people you know that always have a funny take on life and spend some time laughing with them. Or watch some side-splitting funny movies, with people who love to have a good time, pop on the popcorn (yes I enjoy popcorn, it doesn't have too many calories if it's not drenched in butter). Spend a few hours laughing. You might be surprised at how your problems appear less dramatic and manageable after this little activity. Try it.

We've talked about respite from a natural perspective, so let's look at God's view on it. Biblical rest.

God's rest and peace

My world changed dramatically when I began to think about God and visualise Bible verses. It was like visiting with my Heavenly Father. From the edge of burnout, my miraculous recovery commenced. I began to feel relaxed, rejuvenated and as a result changes began inwardly. I was motivated by the fear of burnout and as a result I had to make a determined effort. I had to be quiet and set time aside from the rat race of my life.

> *"If we want to hear God's voice, the first thing we need to be is quiet. God won't shout above the cacophony of our lives. God will come to you in a gentle whisper. But you'll never hear God's voice unless you turn off the noise. "Be still and know that I am God."*[27]

He longs for us to connect with Him and He's available whenever we are. Things can change radically by simply making the commitment to stop for a few minutes and enter into God's peace. This can change us personally and as a wonderful bonus also positively affects and influences those around us.

Come close to God, and God will come close to you ...[28]

It was some years ago that I stopped and took time out to be with God. He honoured that sacrifice of time given to Him. Giving up some of my busyness and offering that time to Him instead, meant that He and I could *rub shoulders* and He could *rub off* onto me. It was a Holy Spirit operation and it worked like a miracle. It *was* a miracle.

Since that time, I now regularly spend time in my day, quietly resting in Him. I'm addicted and it's fantastic and there are no terrible side effects, only good ones. And I've read, prayed and researched since that time to work out exactly why it's had such a profound effect on my life and countless others. Here are a few things I've learned.

God's very interested in rest and peace as rest is mentioned over 500 times in the Bible and in translating the Hebrew and Greek words is often interchangeable with the word peace. It's interesting isn't it, that God is telling in this small (but also rather enormous) truth, that rest equates with peace. In other words, how should we as humans achieve *peace?* Get some rest.

In the Old Testament rest is described as the Sabbath, or to leave or cease work or relax; Nuwach to withdraw alone and remain quiet; and Shaqat to be quiet, still and settled.[29] These describe a peaceful, physical and mental state. I want some of that for my life. God is so interested in rest that He took a break when creating the world!

> *On the seventh day God had finished his work of creation, so he rested from all his work.*[30]

I believe God sees resting not as a luxury but a necessity, especially if He did it. If God needs to rest occasionally, who are we kidding if we think we don't need to do the same?

In the New Testament, *Anapowo* is to take rest and be refreshed; *Loypoy* is to remain; and *Katapowo/sis* is to stop, rest and settle down.[31] In Hebrews chapter 4 it says that we are to do our **best** to enter into this restful state. And peace, which is one of the fruits of the spirit (*eirene*[32]), also means quietness and rest.

> *... the Holy Spirit produces this kind of fruit in our lives: love, joy, peace, patience, kindness, goodness, faithfulness, gentleness, and self-control.*[33]

From these Bible gems, it seems obvious that God wants you to take some rest and that it will cause some beneficial results within us to enable us to be a godly influence. We seem to have left out the 'rest' part of the Christian equation. We can have all the knowledge and revelations possible but if we're operating from tiredness or exhaustion then it's difficult to operate well. As with any area of our life, God has a way for us to outwork and execute it wonderfully, for the very best outcome.

We all yearn for peace in our lives. You can use God's Word or what are, in effect, His love letters to you to receive time out from hectic. Jesus stopped and rested when He went alone to pray. For Him this was a necessity in His life. You and I as His girls also need to rest to receive some peace. His peace is a supernatural peace that exceeds anything else and that, as we come close to Him, overflows to us.

> *I'm leaving you with a gift – peace of mind and heart. And the peace I give is a gift the world cannot give. So don't be troubled or afraid.*[34]

Finding peace within a God connection will help you face your mountains! You'll be better for the mental and physical interval. To be in God's presence, taking a break increases its effectiveness, helping to refresh you in a few minutes. It's in this haven of security, comfort and love that you can put aside your worries for a time.

This supernatural peace can be accessed by His Words to us. It's a process of meditating on those Words in His love letter to us – the Bible. I will go into more detail about meditation in the next chapter.

At this point we understand that God's desire is for us to spend time dwelling in His Word, so that His voice can be heard in the inner heart in the midst of the outer madness of our world.

This chapter might have been a wake-up call for you. Perhaps it's time to take stock and look objectively at what fills your days and make some decisions to include healthy boundaries, say no, get some sleep, laugh and schedule restful down time.

From a position of being willing to change, in the next chapter you will receive practical strategies and the nitty-gritty of personal de-stress that could just change your life … you becoming the superb vessel of His divine peace and love, pouring into the lives of others you know, making your world and theirs a better place to live.

You can learn how to find peace by taking meditative rest based on Christian scripture. How good is that?

before and after

Sheree, to all who knew her was a tower of strength to those who needed help. In her work Sheree counselled and supported people in high-risk situations. At church she was always ready and willing to volunteer and assist when required. However inwardly, Sheree suffered from low self-esteem, blurred boundaries, anxiety and depression, was often tired, stressed and negatively affected by her clients' personal struggles. She didn't deal well with personal or time boundaries which were beginning to take their toll on every area of her life. She had previously tried everything humanly possible to resolve her issues but without any lasting change.

When her family began to complain, she recognised that it was time for some changes.

The first thing that she did was to begin to completely depend on God to help her. As a result she enlisted some assistance and support from trusted people in her world to hold her accountable to make some decisions and select new choices about how to change.

With this help she recognised her need for healthy boundaries with family, friends, ministry and clients. This wasn't an easy transition but from recognition she realised that enough was enough and she knew that for change to occur, she had to change.

She began to cross off some items from her must-do list. Many were worthy tasks, but some not essential. Others needed to (and did) step up to the mark and take ownership. To make this change she learnt to gently say *no* with consideration for both herself and others.

She focussed on getting more sleep, scheduled some family and friend fun time to laugh and enjoy life again. And importantly, she allocated specific personal downtimes to rest with God for her much-needed replenishment, recovery and peace.

Sheree is still on this journey but is consistently making ground. She writes:

> "I've always known how important it is to stop, be still and attend to God regularly but had always struggled with putting this into practice so had major problems with depression and anxiety. I decided that no more of my life would be wasted on lack of boundaries, or being anxious and stressed, so I began to get help. This is where real changes occurred. It was difficult to break lifelong habits and behaviours, but with support, guidance, encouragement, wisdom and strategic planning I was kept accountable and behaviours did change ... I am extremely grateful ... "

2 – getting off the treadmill

Get ready to put in place some action to take much needed rest, and receive God's peace to take your life back. Just like Sheree did.

short and sweet

- Self care is looking after ourselves so that we can care for those we care about, Mat. 22:37-39.
- Busyness in today's society is like a badge of honour.
- Slow down, perhaps do things another way or even God's way.
- God's timing is best. Now moments are to be enjoyed, Eccl. 3:1.
- Your tomorrows are the result of your planning and believing today, Heb.11:1, 3.
- Set some realistic goals for what you believe God wants to achieve through you, Phil. 3:12-14.
- Take breaks. They are health giving and allow for recuperation.
- Constant doing-ness causes constant pressure. Don't ignore the need to rest; take regular breaks, Ex. 33:14; Ps. 127:2.
- Personally take charge to break the cycle of constant activity.
- Saying no and setting boundaries are healthy for you and others, Matt. 7:6.
- Helping others in difficulty and being helped in return is biblical, but we are also meant to carry our own personal loads with the Lord's help, Matt. 11:28.
- Saying sorry, no, allows others to take personal ownership and reap their own consequences, Gal. 6:7-8; 2 Cor. 9:6.
- God designed rest to replenish our reserves. It allows our body to recover. Recreation and holidays,

- although beneficial for well-being, are not the same as body recovery, Gen. 2:2.
- The key is having a good balance of activities, Eccl. 3:1.
- Sleep is essential, God designed and most of us need 7-8 hours a day. Missing sleep can cause severe impairment, Ps. 127:2; Isa. 29:10.
- Anxiety, depression or night-time adrenaline highs can make sleep difficult, Prov. 3:24; Eccl. 5:12.
- Some sleep strategies include: reduced anxiety and increased peace before sleep; a regular routine; daytime exercise; reducing stimulants before bed; sorting out problems before night; trusting God for sleep; meditating on God, His Word and His acts in your life, Ps. 3:5; Ps. 4:8; Rom. 8:28.
- Try intentional laughter and happiness as a short-term anti-depressant and a long term habit for a lifetime, Neh. 8:10; Ps. 126:2-3, 5.
- God's rest and peace are often used interchangeably in the Bible and we are to do our best to achieve it, Heb. 4:11; Jam. 4:8.
- Finding peace within a God connection will help you face your mountains, Isa. 52:7.

journey journaling

- Ask for His help and direction on this journey.
- Who could you be accountable to: who would support any godly changes you decide to make?
- Describe or draw a picture of a peaceful you. What are some small steps you could start right away?

- Ask God for His perspective on your busyness.
- With whom do you need to set some healthy boundaries? What would these look like?
- When you rest, is your body recovering or are you still busy in your rest activities? What can you do to change this?
- Can your sleep improve? List some strategies to improve your peace levels before bedtime.

a prayer

Father God, the Bible tells us that you made Heaven and Earth and then You rested on the seventh day. I know also from the Bible that Jesus, You often left Your earthly responsibilities to pray and rest so I'm reminded to do the same. Forgive me for thinking I can follow You without taking time out with You, to find my peace and restoration in You.

Lead and help me to choose wisely regarding stopping, saying no, having more joy and taking rest. Thank You, Lord, Amen.

3 — stress less

In the previous chapter we talked about the importance of caring for ourselves, creating healthy boundaries and taking rest breaks. God designed rest, sleep and laughter – all of which can help you live a more balanced life.

In this chapter I will describe strategies to assist you to create peaceful downtime in your busy life. This method has been road-tested on many women in workshops and in my coaching practice. I have aimed to teach them how to implement a Christian meditation technique, and literally change their lives for the better.

You also could be changed if you were to put some of the ideas contained here, into practice. You too could become a small but significant drop in the ocean, sending out beautiful influencing ripples of peace and harmony that intersect with and impact the lives of others.

a God moment

My pre-burnout life and influence was at the best of times a little chaotic, subtly affecting those in my world. At worst, it resembled my flooded laundry, something that occurred in my home several times when I was a young mum and washing machines required more attention and work. The spills created would leave the floor ankle-deep in a pond that flowed from room to room. Like my periodic laundry catastrophes, my life sometimes spilled and flooded my 'living' rooms, pouring out irritation and frustration.

So what changed? What was it that God gently spoke deep within me as burnout loomed yet again? I felt He spoke this way: *Peta, take time away from what you're doing and sit with me often so that I can refresh you. My response? How do I fit that in too, God?*

But I was desperate and not up to arguing. So I was

willing to try anything, even something as simple as this. I had a lot to gain but much more to lose if I sank into the void of burnout once again.

So right there and then I put my life on hold. I stopped my thoughts from dwelling on the million and one things that had hijacked them, and sat awhile thinking about God. I sought just *Him*, His peace, His love.

It felt unusual and a little strange. But somehow it also felt restful. I began to regularly and mostly on the hour, wander out to the restroom, or go to a spot where I was alone. For five or 10 minutes I'd focus on God. I felt better, almost immediately. But there was more to come.

I realised some months later that there had been significant inward and outward change when my doctor's receptionist told me of a comment he made to her earlier about me: "Peta is like a walking antidepressant, fun to be around and to treat."

I was at first surprised by the comment. Then as I thought about her words, the enormity of what was actually happening to me below the surface, blew me away. I realised that there was a by-product of this increasing inner peace in my life. And that was the *real* me. The one that God designed with my sense of fun and humorous chit-chat had been released to impact others. The heaviness that I had carried for years had been reduced to such an extent that I as the unique God-created individual, could at long last get going. Soon I knew that what I was learning was of immense value for other women. Particularly for those who yearn to be an influence for God, but don't know what to do or where to start. Peace is a good start!

A lot of water has flowed under the bridge since those days. Good, gently flowing ripples of God-inspired influence. Since those early days many women have also experienced similar and for them wonderful, results.

In a nutshell the process is about resting in God and allowing His supernatural peace to work within. At the very least, allowing our minds and bodies to take a regular breather is a good thing for our physical health. And at its very best, God's miraculous touch is available for us to receive power, life, connection and peace.

a touch of God

Over the years as I and others have mastered this process of resting, I've prayerfully refined it to include the safety of scripture. I believe that the Bible is inspired by God[1] so that the words in it can be and should be our vehicle for living. Using those words in a meditative way is powerful. Otherwise the mind could go off on a tangent that isn't helpful. Despite medical and scientific advances, the human brain and mind is still only partially understood. We do know, however, that the brain continually works with little or no down time, even in sleep.[2] For this reason, it's important to support our rest and focus our mind on biblical verses that are His love letters to us.

Some women are stressed, anxious, in need of peace, or on the edge of burnout as I was. You might be one of these women, so the process I'm about to describe could be an answer to finding that peace. Taking time out in this way – in short moments of God-inspired-peace – I have named God Moments. That's just what it is – creating a few spaces within the haste of our days to spend some time with, and be touched by God. It's taking a leave of absence from everything else that continually draws us … replaced by a moment with Him.

For me, close to burnout once again all those years ago, it meant a dramatic alteration in my way of living. I was in such a bad state of anxiety and hopelessness that this was needed quickly. So I began to stop - on the hour, every hour. To leave whatever it was that I was doing (this includes working, cooking, even interacting with others if possible) to take myself off by myself. These God moments had a dramatic effect within a very short time so that I became committed to continuing these times. The alternative was my motivation (MMs from chapter 2).

For you, depending on the urgency (or not) of need for stress relief, you may find every hour is not achievable. If this is the case, I recommend you begin trying to take a break at least once every day around the same time (more if you can), to create a new habit. Get some accountability if you need to – someone to help you get started ... and stick at it.

To get the most from taking some time out, let this time be about encountering God and His presence. To simply wait on Him without an agenda. This might seem hard at first, but stay with me for some strategies on how to do that towards the end of this chapter. Let this time be about being with God rather than doing or thinking. In time it is possible to be more aware of Who He Is, in greater and more meaningful ways.

> *Oh, how great are God's riches and wisdom and knowledge! His ways!*[3]

meditation is biblical

At some time, you or someone you know, has probably been involved in some kind of meditation training program in a workplace or educational institution. Yoga and other Eastern mindfulness techniques are now all the rage. And there are now many courses being offered through local councils in order to assist people to manage the increase in daily stresses. Stress management is also now a regular inclusion in tertiary curriculum. As an educator for many years, I personally taught this topic in a range of teaching disciplines.

Why is it that there is an increase in meditative practice? It could be that these techniques have been found to physically alter the brain centres that regulate emotions[4], thereby positively affecting feelings. There is increasing research highlighting the benefits of meditative practice assisting the management of chronic pain, improving energy levels as well as lowering depression and anxiety.[5]

Meditation however, is not a new concept. In fact it is a biblical term mentioned 20 times in both old and new Testaments of the Bible. Let me repeat, meditation is biblical rather than a New-Age invention.

The biblical Greek translates meditation as *to ponder, think about* and *imagine*[6] God, His Word and His actions. You might want to read those italicised words once again. If we take those words in the literal sense, (and I'm no Bible scholar but Strong's concordance makes me appear clever), it is therefore probably okay to visualise and imagine Bible verses, seeing them in our mind's eye as a visual sense. I hope it fits with your theology. If not, then allowing Bible words to flow through the mind would be the next best thing to the visualisation of the verses.

It is also absolutely biblically fine to think about Who God is and what His actions are like. Remember that meditation simply means to ponder, think about and imagine: God, His Word and/or His acts. For you, this may mean remembering when He came through for you in the past, (His acts). Or it could mean to picture Him with you in a scene that a verse conjures up in your mind, (imagining). Or you could slowly and gently mentally repeat a verse, (think about His Word).

Study this Book of Instruction continually. Meditate

on it day and night ... Only then will you prosper and succeed in all you do.[7]

The first step to a new habit is a decision. To get it firmly in place takes practice and dedication. Putting in a new habit of de-stress meditation (having a God Moment) is no different. It will take determination as many other tasks call us away.

discipline and focus

Habits are only produced by repetition and a commitment to create changed results by changing our actions. A lot is at stake; a peaceful and perhaps transformed life. And as mentioned in the previous chapter, your relationships, physical well-being, clear thinking and a host of other benefits can be the result of reducing stress.

It will take firmness to a new way of doing things to set aside time and focus on new thoughts. But by taking necessary recovery time for the health of your body and soul, whilst focussing on God's peace, rather than the worries of the world, will bring results if consistently applied. I've seen the proof of this time and time again with the countless women I have taught this method to over many years.

In a way I guess I've been practising, refining and perfecting the method using myself and my wonderful clients. I've come up with three simple steps, each Biblically based. These together form a single meditative process that I call God Moments (GMs). God Moments can put a stop to us sliding into hyper-stress levels.

I will separate and explain the three parts in detail shortly but to summarise here, the full preventative process consists of slowly *breathing* to settle; then casting our cares and handing them to God, something I call *dumping*. And finally the last step is resting and being still in God's presence. Each one of these steps work together as a complete GM or used individually as stand alone '*minis*', or reactive GMs for fast relief of stress.

However you might decide to use it, the technique is quite simple but will probably take time to put into practice. With my experience working with clients I have found that it can take 3 to 6 months to reduce high levels of stress and have a solid habit in place.

So if you want to make some changes to achieve peace in your life, set some time aside and let's get started.

slow your breathing!

To help settle down from thoughts and busyness, it's a good idea to slow down your breathing, which is calming in and of itself. If you begin with just this each day, stress can be reduced to some degree. Start by slowly inhaling, taking in and holding the air for a second in the lungs before slowly exhaling. This helps relax and settle the body and mind. (Please check with your doctor if you have any medical conditions.)

You can picture (meditate on) God's breath that creates life (mentioned in Gen. chapter 2). In this chapter, God made man from the dust of the Earth but it wasn't until He breathed life into the man's body (see verse 7) that man came alive. In a way this is true of our journey with God. We are alive if our heart is beating, but in a spiritual sense 'dead' until we know Jesus as our Lord. Then we become *new* (see 2 Cor. 5:17).

Consider then each breath that we take, millions of them in a single lifetime. Easy to take for granted but each breath presents us another moment on this Earth. They are God's gift of life and how wonderful, the process of simply taking a breath. And then another. And another. As we can gently focus on each one, they can become a special moment with our Creator.

You can start now by sending up a quick prayer to God to receive His life with each breath. Try now, as you slow your breathing, to focus on that life being breathed into you, as you slowly breathe in, hold it and slowly exhale. Imagine (it's biblical) His breath of life that we know from science will turn into life-giving oxygen as it enters the blood stream to move through your body. In your mind's eye, picture this movement of air becoming oxygen moving from your nose then lungs to your whole body. Picture each part of your body receiving God's life as you exhale. So it looks like this. Breathe in God's breath of life as you slowly inhale. Hold it, then slowly exhale and imagine God's life moving down through each part of your body.

Take about three to four slow breaths or up to 10 if you have the time available. With each one visualise the life in the form of oxygen moving from the top of your body to the extreme body ends such as your fingers and toes. This thinking, as well as visually seeing God's life (oxygen) in you, helps focus on something other than daily concerns. Breathing deeply is also beneficial physically as it creates a maximum dose of oxygen into the lungs. This can lower blood pressure which may help reduce some of that tension you've been carrying around for way too long.

As well as beginning a God Moment, this focussed and slowed breathing on its own is also a great mini de-stress on-the-run because you can do this with your eyes open or closed. Great for those times in the car whilst stopped at red lights, or in the bathroom, or seated waiting for your computer to boot up. There are a million and one different opportunities and places for you to *keep breathing* in God's flow of life.

Once you have slowed your breathing, we need to address the never-ending stream of thoughts, cares or concerns, that we as women have racing around our head!

I call it dumping.

dump your junk

This is the second step in the three parts of a GM. It's where we can stand aside from our worries for a few moments. Sound good? Most women that I work with think this is not possible. However, it is not only doable but a part of Cognitive Based Therapy (CBT). CBT is a well-respected and researched therapy which can assist to reduce ruminating or letting negative thoughts take over.[8] Christianity has its own CBT, and it's as old as the hills and very successful! We can take our thoughts captive[9] by replacing negative thinking with uplifting positive God thoughts, bringing them into line with His Word. As women we know this but generally don't find it easy to do. I don't know about you but I generally have countless thoughts racing around in my head, so to take my thoughts captive is for me, not easy. Visualising the process of dumping makes the process easier.

Often in my seminars I have volunteers perform a visual play-on-words to show how this could work in a practical sense. One girl plays Jesus with arms outstretched; another is the Father sitting on His throne. A third girl acts out the Holy Spirit floating along behind Ev, short for 'every' woman! Ev is bent almost double, carrying a huge pack of heavy items. Due to its size the baggage becomes a barrier to getting close to God. The Holy Spirit however assists and helps her to discard each item one-by-one. Even the good things like dinner menus (a cookery book is discarded from the backpack) and making love with hubby (sexy underwear is extracted from the bag, it always gets a laugh). Stuff that is keeping us stressed or too busy to think clearly, is given into God's hands or at the feet of Jesus. The play ends when all Ev's baggage is emptied, she stands up straight and free and can then share a group hug with the Father, Son and Holy Spirit. In other words, as she gives Him all her burdens to carry, she can get close to God.

This illustration makes a strong point that in a spiritual sense our emotions, busyness or baggage – no matter how well intended or worthy – sometimes stop us from a deeper relationship with God.

He wants to take over our worries. If only we can give them up for a time, He'll willingly take them and work miracles in them if we let them go.

God cares for you, so turn all your worries over to him. [10]

Cast your burden on the Lord [releasing the weight of it] and He will sustain you ... [11]

My future is in your hands. [12]

To start the dumping process of handing over your worries, picture yourself giving any stuff, or baggage, even your 'good' plans or intentions, one at a time into His loving hands. The second scripture above tells us to release the weight of it. How often have we given things to God only to pick them right back up soon after? If you can imagine taking the weight of your worries completely from your shoulders and giving them away, it's a wonderful feeling. The challenge is to leave them with God and not pick them up again straight away. Right? But I am challenged by this. I have to remind myself that I'm handing these things over to God for just a few minutes, allowing Him to do in that time what we couldn't achieve in a lifetime.

Dealing with the issue of sin can be visual; you could visualise nailing sins or placing them at the foot of the cross.[13] You might have to do some business with God such as forgiving others before you dump (covered in the next section, *Freedom & Influence*). When I teach spiritual meditation classes to unchurched people, I suggest a tip-up-truck or large skip (dumpmaster) for dumping. Ladies report back they've dumped all sorts of things from bills to ex-husbands in the dumpmaster! The visuals are incredible aren't they? Whichever picture you choose, I suggest starting with a verse (remember scripture is safe), and seeing it in your mind's eye as you imagine it playing out.

If we allow God to take hold of our issues, He can transform them and us. Just for a short while, as we dump, we can emotionally step aside for a little while to allow God to work on our troubles.

Once your stuff is dumped or given to God, the next part of a full GM is to really connect with God and just *be*.

being with God

Handing over the reins of control during this part of a GM is really the key to successful resting in a GM.

To be, we need to learn to completely let go and give up. I talk more on control in the next section of the book. For now, it's important to allow God to be God rather than you or me trying to organise and control our world.

If you are anything like me, to give over control is a continual challenge, the result being a probable spillover into the de-stressing routine. It is often a reason why some women find it difficult to relax during the GM process. As you surrender that control again and again, giving situations and relationships to God's ways, it becomes possible to know the beginning of real surrender and freedom in Christ.[14]

To do that, when the thinking wanders or begins to plan, sort, organise, (in other words control our world), don't panic and be jolted away from the place of peace. Breaking an old habit and rewiring the brain whilst making a new one will take some time. Be patient!

To assist the process of *being*, I have a couple of scriptures that I often use myself and also teach from. When I'm finding one is becoming a bit 'dry' or I don't seem able to connect as well as I had in the past, I'll change verses, finding one that God seems to be speaking to me in my now. This can change depending on our life challenges at any time and believe me we all have them, don't we? For a full list of verses that I suggest, see appendix 1.

The key to relaxing *in* God is to 'be there' *with* God. Offer up a quick prayer for His help to just be. Then using a selected verse, listen to the words forming naturally or rolling over in your brain and watch the picture that forms in your mind as on a video screen.

Here's my all-time favourite that I come back to over and over again. As it's a popular one with many that I teach, I'll go into the meaning of the words in depth. I hope you will receive a revelation into your heart to help you *go* and *be* in that place with Him.

Be still, and know that I am God ... [15]

The word *'Be'* or *'Be-ing'* is all about experiencing God's presence in the now. In the present moment (see chapter 1). However in the middle of GM de-stress, thoughts will often wander to what happened yesterday or what's for dinner. Life-changing stuff perhaps not, but it's these small decisions that keep our minds active. Or perhaps we might have some pressing challenging issues or decisions to make. The interruptions might be our thoughts on how this will work. How can *I* make it work? That's been a difficult one for me and others too. So just continue to focus. Remember, it's important.

Taking a GM is about *stillness* for a short period of time. The Hebrew word for still is *raphah* which translated means to stay, cease or slacken.[16] This is all about being present and ceasing what we're doing or thinking. But how on Earth is this remotely possible? If you think about it, when do you stop? Really stop? Don't give up on me yet. The next words might help you get a picture that you can watch, visualise and meditate on.

In this verse, at the same time as we stop what we are doing, we have to do something else that is just as important as stopping! It's to recognise and be familiar with God or to 'Know'! This word in Hebrew is Yada, meaning to *know* intimately, to see, to care, to be *aware of*.[17]

Knowing someone or something is to be certain and assured of who or what we know. It's something we have experienced. It's personal and its revelation to our insides. The Bible calls this our heart. It's different to knowing *about* Him. It's about knowing Him experientially. To know my husband after many years of marriage is to understand that when he holds his face a certain way, or speaks with a particular tone of voice, I'm aware of his mood or his feelings. This happens over a period of time, in this case years as I've learnt more about him and know him better.

It's similar with God. When we meet this amazing, incredible God, the experience is so beautiful that we want to know more of Him. If you don't know Him, it's as simple as going to Him with an open believing heart and making Him your friend. (See my story in Appendix 2.)

Don't for a minute believe that God is too busy to concern Himself with your seemingly insignificant day-to-day problems. God is interested in the small and the larger issues in our everyday lives and longs to have you with Him. Know that you are important and valuable to God and that you have a royal position as a child of the King.

> ... *seated us with him in the heavenly realms* ... [18]

As you wait on Him you will begin to recognise how important you are to Him and His love for you. You will understand that you can go to Him as often as you need to simply sit quietly with Him. The power of this part of a GM, sitting quietly, expectantly, cannot be overstated. Women from all seasons of life report radical changes in their lives as they begin to be in God's presence regularly. They report a new excitement about getting into His presence; reading His Word, doing His will and a love for others. If you want that, it is worth the effort.

Once we know God by meeting and accepting Jesus and we connect again and again, there's a peace in His presence that passes any earthly or human understanding.[19]

the Lord is my shepherd

Back to the verse, *Be still and know that I am God.* The word 'God' is about recognising God's immensity and vastness. It's recognising that God is God of our lives and everything created and we are not! He is the all-powerful all-knowing Creator of the universe! The Great I am![20] He desires to be close and intimate with us.

In the GM process, connecting during this time is to remember that beautiful connection you had with Him during worship on Sunday, or this morning when praying or on your morning walk recognising God's creation. Or perhaps it's going to the scene that this Scripture brings to mind. It's about the experience, the knowing of the all-time Creator.

This heavenly connection is where true peace is found in a spiritual sense. In the physical, it's where our body can receive true and longed-for body recovery as the heart rate slows and cortisol levels drop. Happiness and optimism can also be the result.[21]

How good is that? Not only can we meet with our Creator and receive His love and peace but our bodies can react in the way they were made to. Our body can perform all the processes necessary for healthy living with the switching on of the stress hormones occasionally in emergency situations, rather than continually due to constant busyness.

The other verses that I often use personally for the final part of the GM process are from the beautiful Psalm 23:

> *The Lord is my shepherd; I shall not want. He makes me to lie down in green pastures; He leads me beside the still waters. He restores my soul ...* [22]

The whole psalm is a beautiful analogy of how to live life, but we're going to dig into the deeper meanings of the first couple of verses. As we meditate on these words in our GM process after breathing and dumping, we get a picture of Jesus, the Shepherd of our soul and our lives. We do not need anything because He is and has all that we need for life in Him alone (v.1).

In verse 2, notice the word *makes* used in the KJV (which is a very accurate translation of the original Hebrew). We need to be *made* to lie down and take a rest just like those sheep that David wrote about. God certainly had to *make* me rest and lie down through the uncomfortable result of burnout. What about you? Are you at the point where it feels like He's almost cornered you to take a break for your own good and those around you? I still have to almost force myself to stop for my own good at times when my heart is racing and I feel that surge of adrenalin. So I usually say this verse in my head, reminding myself that He's helping me to stop and is making me rest.

What do you see when you read the rest of verse 2? Make a mental note or better still write down the scene with as much detail as possible to help you remember that sense of serenity at those times when you rest. Include the grass, the sky, the greenery and of course the water. Just thinking about this scene produces a beautiful sense of peace even now as I write. The next verse speaks of calming restoration for your soul. What does that look like for you? Write down what you see and how you feel.

The process of having a GM is a serene way to meditate in God's presence. But it will take more than just a decision, it will take grit!

persevere

Just *be*-ing. So simple in essence, but not so easy to do. This final part of the full process is to connect with God. I hear you say, *I wish!* This seems so difficult for most people, especially us women because we rarely stop to smell the roses, let alone listen to God's voice. It will take practice and perseverance, with big doses of patience for you to learn to do this naturally. But it will happen with time if you keep trying and don't give up on it. I'm often asked to coach people through this time of making a new habit because it seems just too hard to settle and connect at this point.

It's the making of new neural circuitry, or creating something in your brain from nothing whilst moving into a place of peace that is so challenging. If you realise that incredible physical and emotional recovery can result from the reduction of chronic stress hormone production in your body, you should be able to push through. The fantastic thing is that your normal body functions such as digestion, creative thinking, immune functioning (to name just a few) will kick in, if you can just remove some stress.[23]

peace anywhere, anytime

To get the most from taking GMs, consider the two reasons for pressing through the hard times when it seems you can't find the motivation to put in this new habit:

1. Preventative GMs keep you calm before any problems arise. It's good to plan two per day so that you are ready for anything!

2. Reactive GMs (minis) help you to calm down amid high stress or impossible situations. I used to find that at dinner time I would get annoyed and hassled, everyone wanting a piece of me.

3. Think about some possible times to regularly take GMs then begin.

Consider some time prompts in your days where you can set aside time to regularly take a moment with God, then set your mind to do it with whatever prompts will work for you. They might include by the clock, or before or after meals, or times when the kids are engaged or at school or with other family members.

- Put some relaxing music – preferably instrumental – on your iPod or phone and have it playing in the background as you take some de-stress time out on the run;

- Set your alarm clock for 5 or 10 minutes, then have a GM. You know you have 5 minutes of no interruptions before you recommence your schedule;

- When someone irritates you, before you answer back with something you may be sorry for later, zip the lip, excuse yourself for a moment, park yourself somewhere, (on the toilet seat if you must. I think I know all the toilets in my area as I've taken time out on my busy travels). Once away, take-two! 2 minutes that is! On your return, your answer will probably be peppered with grace and forgiveness. Rubbing shoulders with the Great I Am can't help but change and soften even the hardest of hearts.

And let me say that the more you practise, the better you will get at recognising when you need a break. Your brain with new peace circuitry will read you and your stress-related responses better as it recognises the difference between your body at peace or overstressed. You will recognise when you need to relax after months of having GMs.

Find different places. All you need is about 10 minutes several times each day. To begin building a habit, try for one per day, then build up to more. To find a spot in the busyness of womanhood, be creative and proactive – use the toilet seat to best advantage against marauding and hungry 2-year-olds or teens who must be driven everywhere right away!

And then you can grab a mini anywhere, anytime and for as long or as short a time as required or desired. You can use any part of the three parts, breathe, dump or be as stand-alone de-stress experiences. However, most find that the full three-part GMs are the most beneficial for real rest and two or more of these each day (I'm a stress-head and I need a minimum of 3 and up to 10 every single day to prevent madness and mayhem!)

Use the suggestions below to take quick GM breaks in your day wherever you are. These ones might be short minis rather than the full, breathe, dump and be. Use any of these that will work for you, from several deep breaths feeling God's life move down your body to dumping your junk in God's hands. Or just being still, remembering that connection you had with Him previously. All will go a long way to settle you and keep you smelling like fresh roses rather than a grumpy old (or young) woman. Opportunities for taking mini GMs include while:

- Drying your hands with blow driers at public conveniences
- Waiting in queues at the bank or other places
- Waiting for the computer to boot up, have some beautiful and relaxing scenery on your desktop
- Waiting for your phone call to be answered
- In the bathroom (you get the idea probably)
- Sitting with a cuppa, waiting for it to cool
- Sitting at traffic lights in the car
- Before driving after school drop-off time
- Waiting in the car at school pick-up time
- Travelling by public transport
- In a park at lunchtime or in the car with doors locked, sunnies on and seat reclined
- Stopping at a park before you begin to drive or before you get out of the car at your destination
- As a passenger whilst someone else is driving
- In the ad breaks watching TV
- Waiting for the kettle to boil
- After finishing one task at your desk, computer or home duties before starting another

From just a few minutes a couple of times each day, whenever possible, taking these short focussed breaks may change the way you do life as you begin to connect with the Almighty God. As you change to become more like

God, the person you are becoming – in other words the real you that God designed – begins to overflow as you positively influence others in your world.

GM tips

Remember to focus on God, in your being connecting time, especially if there is a lot going on and it's difficult to concentrate. If that's difficult, bring back to mind the last time you connected and simply remember what that was like.

Don't try to be too perfect in your connecting with God. There's loads of grace available and He doesn't expect perfection. He's happy you're trying to meet with Him and will honour your heart. He'll meet with you as you relax and not try too hard.

Need a creative idea? Nothing is happening in the brain department? Take a GM, as the alpha brainwaves state that is produced during deep relaxation, can typically release the brain to produce creative solutions that only the left and right brain working together rested, can perform.[24]

Generally, the busier and more stressed you feel, the more impossible to spend the time taking a little break and the more you absolutely need to do it. When under pressure we subconsciously and erroneously believe that if we push through to get the job/s done, the less pressure will be felt. Wrong! I have found the exact opposite to be true. The more we go-go-go, the more stressed we become and then the more we push and the worse we work. It's a never-ending cycle.

Instead, taking regular breaks even 10 minutes every hour, can make us more productive, efficient and clear-headed. As a general rule, *the more stressed, the more blessed from* having a GM.

In Appendix 1 you will find a variety of verses that you might like to use at some time. Each one has its own beauty and I have found they help me connect with God at various times in my walk of life away from stress. Different verses will help you at different times. I suggest that you keep them handy wherever you take your breaks. That way you can refer to any one of them if you find it difficult to connect with your current GM verse.

Periodically, GMs need a tweak when you feel your mind begins to wander as a result of over familiarisation with a verse that has previously been helpful. It may then be time to introduce in a new scripture so that the God-connection is fresh and vibrant.

Prepare your de-stress zones to make it relatively easy to get away and begin the habit.

Think about those times in the day that will work for you and how you will fit this into your life. This generally requires some thought.

A well-placed chair, letting the kids know as well as your husband or your significant others. I have a friend who is completing a master's degree with four children and a husband that works away in the mines in WA. When she's getting frazzled her kids often notice it before she does and tell her to go off by herself *(to breathe mum)*. She is glad she does and so are they. You and those you care about will too.

the overflow

You and I are on the planet to shine the Light. It's a never-ending flow within us as we connect with our Maker in order to be a flow to the world.

Usually, we're too tired or irritable to be anything but a worn-out or burnt-out old candle wick (speaking for myself, I wouldn't want to presume you act as irrationally as I do at times). By stopping and getting a connection with God, it is entirely possible to be revitalised and renewed to carry on with new vigour and vitality with God-power.

> ... a lamp is placed on a stand, where its light can be seen by all.[25]

As you begin to enjoy these quiet times, your peace levels may change and your stress levels may begin to diminish. Many women find that health issues and quality of life improves. I also hear many reports of calmer girls who now find it easier to forgive others. God changes us first from the inside which then impacts how we live life and engage in our relationships. Our environments can possibly change as a result of the change in us first.

A new kind of peace that copes better with what is going on in our world can produce a mental shift that encourages us to go to God instead of yelling at the husband or the kids. (It works with me and countless others that have put this connecting with God into place.) The God of the universe, who created you and me brings a higher dimension to our ability to cope. There's an emotional, physical but also spiritual transfer that occurs. And guess what, this changes the environment. That means ... husbands, children, family, neighbours, and even by progression, the world. It's awesome.

A life influenced by the Holy Spirit produces evidence of the fruit of the Spirit in a life. Perhaps, as was the case in my life, this was long elusive to you. But, with ongoing connecting with God, the fruit could become a reality in your life. Love, joy, peace, patience, kindness, goodness, faithfulness, gentleness and self-control,[26] as an ever-flowing overflow from an inner vessel rippling out into an ocean. It's your world and the world beyond that is impacted as a result of your times with Him. Like me you may still occasionally lose your cool at times (overflowing messes) but you now have a strategy to immediately get right and calm once again. Drop by beautiful drop.

It sounds so simple and it is. What isn't so easy however is making the decision to do it again and again or simply remembering to take a moment. We can get so caught up with life that to stop doesn't always seem like an option. But making it a habit is possible with determination as we remember the rewiring potential of our brain.

Using this simple means of moving closer to God, my heartfelt hope for you is that you find that place of peace that resides within you. You can be the incredible godly influence in your husband's, girlfriends', friends', family and neighbours' lives. Your world can change and be like never before. This is God's heart!

> *You and I are God's creative and created masterpieces, specially re-created in Christ Jesus as new, to do all the good things, He planned ..." "... and He will work out His plans for your life ...* [27]

This meditative GM journey is very much worth the cost of your focus, time and commitment to building the habit. So be focussed. Be disciplined. A lot is at stake. Take urgent recovery time for the health of your body and soul. Focus on that urgent need for peace, rather than the worries of the world.

You may find, as others have, that you now have a more spiritually open state of mind. This can be extremely helpful to delve into and uproot any hurt or pain causing life problems. Section 2 will look at some practical tools for Holy Spirit inner healing.

before and after

Living peaceful, stressless lives doesn't come easily for most of us and Tabitha wasn't any different. Her life was busy. As well as the ongoing demands as a wife and mother at home, she also volunteered in a leading role at church and had a professional career. A highly experienced midwife in a large country hospital, she performed extremely important and sometimes life-saving procedures in often time-pressured conditions.

Bringing babies into the world and caring for both mother and new infant required quick thinking and a clear head. Tabitha needed to be able to think clearly, particularly when it came to making life and death decisions with split-second timing.

Tabitha found that stress was making subtle inroads into her work, life and in her relationships with God, her husband and children. She was no longer enjoying her work or her ministry at her church and life itself was becoming drudgery.

Juggling all that her life required of her, she often experienced stress and felt God gently nudging her towards making important changes to the way she handled her nervous energy at work and at the end of her busy days.

She made a decision to put in the strategies described here. She worked hard to find appropriate and achievable slots to de-stress within her busy days, although at first finding those spots seemed impossible. She recognised that it was necessary as the alternative was to keep living the way that she had been – stressed!

Tabitha describes not only how it feels to live stressless but also how the extra and wonderful benefit of GMs or meditation using scripture, is achieving a beautiful closeness with God – as His peace helps us deal with stress. She began to hear His voice without a tangle of jumbled, confused or worried thoughts.

She writes:

> ... I needed to make changes in my life.
>
> I'm not a very spontaneous person and usually have to think things through fairly well before I respond, but once I decided to make those changes, there was no looking back.
>
> I learnt how to rest in God and unburden myself of my worries, handing them over to Him. The mountains that I had ... today no longer exist because of the changes that have happened inside me.
>
> On this journey, I have learnt so many new things about myself, had new revelations on Scripture but most importantly I have grown closer to my Heavenly Father.

short and sweet

- God's peace is a natural way of relieving anxiety for God-girls in today's hectic world, Ps. 46:10; Heb. 4:11.
- Use Bible verses to meditate on, to receive a sense of calm and peace, Ps. 27:4, 77:6, 105:2.
- Meditation is a biblical word so it's okay to think and imagine scriptures, Ps. 63:6, 77:12, 143:5; 1 Tim. 4:15.
- Meditate by thinking about and imagining God, His Word or His acts in your life, Ps. 119:148.
- Be disciplined about learning to de-stress which is about your personal self-care, Acts 24:16, Prov. 5:12.
- God Moments are about breathing, dumping and being in God's restful presence, Ps. 91:1.

- A GM starts with slow breathing, picturing God's breath of life moving through your body, see Gen. 2:7.
- The next part is to dump your junk, which includes any thoughts or concerns, good or bad, 1 Pet. 5:7.
- If your mind wanders, focus and go back to your original God-thoughts, 2 Cor. 10:5.
- Relaxing in God is all about getting so close to Him, and surrendering all over to His control, James 4:8; Ps. 46:10.
- It's about an intimate friendship with the Shepherd of our lives, Ps. 23.
- Finally, being in the moment and sitting in God's presence using a beautiful verse imagining the scene will help you connect with God, Ps. 46:10.
- Take GMs anywhere, everywhere, to prevent stress (preventative GMs) and when stressed (reactive GMs).
- As a general rule, the busier you are and the less time you have, the more you need to have a GM.
- God's peace changes everything from the inside of you to the world beyond, Gal. 5:22-23.
- Peace is for you and for the benefit of others as you spread it around, John 14:27.
- With God's help get started! Pour out the overflow of God's peace, you ripple producer, you!

journal the journey

- Think about the possible times of your days where you can stop. Try to find a time that will work for you each day around certain activities. For example, before or after your shower or breakfast; lunch time; before driving away from work, in the car; once home in your comfy chair and private place before starting the evening activities. Make a commitment to begin. Find someone to be accountable to so as to have support.

- Journal the picture that you see when reading Psalm 23:1-3. Describe the scenery, yourself and the Shepherd to create the 'being' part of a GM.

a prayer

I'm excited Lord by the possibilities of reducing stress and becoming who You designed me to be. Show me how I can begin the journey. I've been running on overdrive for too long.

Forgive me for operating in my own strength rather than in Yours. I want to make some changes and regularly come to You in meditation.

Help me to connect with You during those times so that I can hear You more clearly. Amen.

peta soorkia

SECTION 2

un-frazzled freedom

But the one who plants in response to God, letting God's Spirit do the growth work in him, harvests a crop of real life, eternal life. [1]

... Therefore if the Son makes you free, you shall be free indeed ... [2]

We have a spiritual responsibility as women of influence to be a godly encouragement to those around us. In the last section we looked at rest, peace and meditating on Bible verses to change your inner and outer world, becoming a woman who creates ripples of peace into the vast ocean of life. But we need to be free within to do this successfully. And not with a works mentality but from an inner freedom that is real and authentic.

To achieve this can be a battle to push through the hard stuff. And it might at times be painful to relive difficult circumstances from the past. But as we take small steps, Jesus will be with us, every step of the way.

So this section will firstly prepare you for freedom that is ours as Christ believers, by finding courage, being real, surrendering control and harnessing thoughts. Then you will learn of the issues that steal freedom. And finally you will be given practical strategies to secure true and lasting liberty.

You and I have all that we need, and that's God. As we step out into danger, in the midst of trials and circumstances, others see our bravery in God.

Other people, some women, are watching. Those closest to you and others further away. Looking for answers and waiting for the powerful influence that you possess to change the atmosphere.

4

freedom for starters

influencing well

You and I as God's women positioned in the here and now to impact and influence the planet, may be carrying unnecessary baggage. We need to get free of any such hindrances in order to be a blessing to others.

That means work, and hard work at that. There is a battle being waged in the heavenlies to keep you locked up and not free. It may be challenging but God is patient and gracious with us as we take small, incremental steps. In our churches there are godly people to support us and we have the Holy Spirit pointing to the ripple-Maker Himself, Jesus. He will be with you and me, every step of the way.

And we have all that we need. God's supernatural power working as we allow it. Sometimes that may mean stepping out into unknown or what to us seems dangerous territory. But by doing that and being in danger, others see our bravery coming from God. It may come as a revelation from God's heart to yours and then reaching out to others. For instance, those closest to you, in your home (partner, child, family member), or in your work (workmate), or in your classroom or neighbourhood. There are those who are waiting for something to change them and help them and it may be you operating in your special abilities to change the atmosphere.

Finding freedom is a process which unfortunately doesn't often happen overnight or in a miraculous instant for most of us. Instead it usually takes some hard work (and mostly a lot of it) on our part whilst also believing for a miracle.

Let's begin with some ways to prepare and start your releasing journey.

courage for change

Jesus told the disciples in Matt. 14:22-32 to go out in the boat and then left them to their own devices, knowing they'd have a circumstance or two called wind, waves and stormy seas. Peter, full of faith after Jesus told him to come, walked on the water – a miracle in the midst of his fear – the storm.

Getting out of the boat is where Jesus wanted Peter and where He wants us too. In our storms we can do as Peter did, call on Jesus, ask for His direction. But recognise that as we go out on a limb, there will be waves and plenty of opportunity to sink. Facing fear is what Peter did when he looked around at where he was. Ok Lord I'm following you out of the boat, shouldn't life be all plain sailing now?

Not necessarily! Walking on water means being prepared to sink. Sink, yes. Drown, no.

Our natural tendency is to stay in the safe zone, so that fear keeps us in the boat! Getting out of our comfort zone, is tough. (Notice Peter was the only disciple who left the boat, see verses 26-30.) But most of us rationalise that it's still safer using our own methods (safe zone) and staying put.

To avoid risky behaviour, some of our safety procedures could be always driving instead of flying or hoarding to avoid running short or even using fly spray excessively to kill any unseen hidden insects. There is a myriad of strategies that you and I use to prevent us being courageous. Preparing is great and necessary but when preparation becomes our answer to our challenges rather than reliance on God, we're in dangerous waters of unbelief and a lack of faith in our God. Our own personal methods become idols to ourselves and our own cleverness. By staying in the boat of security and using those strategies we are safe, largely unchanged and protected (we assume) from the danger of the rough and unknown seas.

However boats are also hazardous as waves can come crashing over and into them, perhaps tipping them – and you if you're hiding there like the other disciples when Peter walked on water – into the raging and open sea. Staying in the boat or where it is seemingly comfortable and safe is therefore perhaps for all of us just as dangerous as getting out into what looks like danger.

I want to get out of my boat – which is my safety net and my limitations. Walking on water is what I want to do. I want to see a change in me to positively affect my circumstances. What about you? What are you afraid of? Is it spiders, financial lack, rejection, heights, relationships, trust, being alone or simply tomorrow that keeps you from getting out?

If you are ready to experience freedom on the water, then you and I need to get real.

digging deep to be real

Sometimes we live our lives pretending, presenting a façade to others which is not authentic. Getting real, or being who we really are without the layers that we build onto our personality, is the key to unearthing freedom. Often these layers cover up the person we are ashamed of.

I had many layers to work through and discard, one by one. The process is a life-long process and well worth the time, effort and even agony sometimes. I hope that what you read and learn in these pages will assist your journey to be simpler and less gruelling than mine. So what was the debris in my life that needed clearing away? As a young person, before I met Christ, I looked in all the wrong places for affirmation and affection. Talk about drugs, sex and rock and roll. I'll spare you the details, but you get the idea.

In the midst of that, my worth was based on the current values (or lack) of the day and gaining attention. So I was conforming, comparing, competing, pretending and perfecting. Underneath, well hidden and way down in case of rejection, was the real me.

Some of my brokenness came from the fact that my sailor father who was away from home a lot of the time and then distant as I came into puberty, died suddenly. I had already felt abandoned and lost and after his untimely death, more so. It took time and it took God to heal me of the pain inside.

Then as an adult, many years later, God gently and lovingly over time has peeled away the layers, of who I was pretending to be. This process began at a day retreat based on encounters developed in Bogata, Colombia, where drug lords, addicts and people with severe problems were finding Christ and being healed by His power at these amazing weekends.

I began to understand that my intense feelings and the ways I had acted, particularly towards men, were the result of my unresolved inner pain. And that freedom from those inner heartaches was indeed possible. As I started to get healing and forgive, the Father's love filled up the emptiness inside. One layer removed. It was the first of many more removed over time that have cut away the pretensions to reveal the person God always meant me to be.

Since that first glimpse of freedom much more has been unloaded in my life. As a minister in personal ministry and in team weekend encounters, I have assisted literally hundreds of people find similar release from their own pain. I have worked in God's supernatural abilities and many times I have seen first hand how God is the miracle restorer.[3]

Are you like many women I have met, who through pain and challenges want to be other than yourself? Yearning or just imagining being like the pastor's wife or the cool girls with their cooler-than-frostbite attitude at school or the other mums with their orderly homes, attentive husbands, trim figures, perfect kids and clothes.

But who are they anyway? Underneath, they probably don't have it together. And who are you on the inside underneath this disguise of perfection?

God desires to lead us towards freedom and our real splendour as we become raw, vulnerable, willing to change and open to His loving correction. In the same way that precious stones are found raw, rough and hidden in lumps of clay rock, we too can be unearthed from our old ways in order to be gloriously refined bit by little bit.

Is it time to dig a bit deeper, to release the person underneath the layers to be who God created you to be? That is the unique you who is being perfected one step and one layer at a time.

As the layers come away, the uncut diamond firstly rough and unpolished, begins to reveal the wonderful secrets of magnificence hidden within. But it requires refining, smoothing and cutting to uncover its loveliness that has been there all along waiting to be revealed. Just like these original gems, in the raw and uncut, with all our insecurities, we are at odds with the godly attributes of grace and love through Christ in us! The process of cutting away refines us (naked – eek!), in the process of de-layering to our true magnificence.

> ... *more precious than jewels ... far above rubies or pearls.*[4]

Since I've grown a little older, my nakedness is not as pretty as when I was a young girl (my hubby says I'm perfect, what a sweetie, lots of brownie points to him). That's because my body is getting somewhat wobbly in places. But nakedness in the spiritual sense is what God requires of us, whatever our 'age' as we mature along our journey.

Do you see yourself as a precious jewel or do you just see your uncut roughness? To clean up the act and peel away the layers, I'm afraid there is a prerequisite step where many of us get stuck. In involves giving something away. It's called control. And it takes surrender. Whoops! Want to give up? Well that's really what's it all about. (Gotcha!)

surrendering control

Sometimes when life takes a worrying turn, I have felt stuck between a rock and a hard place so that I want to give up. Have you felt like this? Our natural tendency is to take the reins and gallop like crazy…be in charge of circumstances, events and people.

We want to be in control of how our husbands behave towards us, how the dishes are done, the bills are paid, the kids act (especially at church, sitting sweetly and definitely no running amok amongst the pews as my kids did) and generally how people in our world deal with us. Giving up control is hard to do as it is often hidden in well-meaning hopes and dreams for ourselves and our families. It is so subtle even though it pervades our self-reliant and perfection-seeking society. I believe most of us women are control freaks trying to be in charge of our world and circumstances.

Why? We are mothers, wives, workers, friends, daughters, neighbours, Christians. We are trying to be everything to everyone but we are probably wearing out in the exertion of it all. This means we are lugging around burdens we were never meant to carry, particularly in the home. Things like the finances, child discipline, spiritual oversight, leadership. If you are a single mum, this is a necessity but weighty all on your own. (Perhaps you can pray for and source a wise male mentor to help you shoulder some of the harder decisions.)

But in fact, only God should have full control of our lives and perhaps he's even allowing difficulties to grow us. Rats! He wants dependence on Him. Letting go of the reins. Letting go of the fear that causes us to control. (See chapter 5 for more on fear, one of the freedom stealers).

God will cause miracle-working power inside us and in our situations as we eventually give up and move to a place of total surrender to Him. When we try to be in control, we are tying God's hands because He will not interfere with our free will. To give up may mean failing occasionally and then getting back up to have another go, whilst learning some lessons in the getting up. And it also means not picking up the pieces after other people's messes so that they can learn to walk their own way.

I meet many women on my speaking travels who tell me they are tired, running on adrenalin and fed up with husbands/kids/others that can't or won't act in the way they want. Instead husbands can't or won't make decisions so the women take control in those areas. It could be disciplining the children, praying together, deciding on schooling, sorting out a problem with the in-laws.

To them and to you I suggest what I've had to do after beating my head against a brick wall trying to get my family to change. Stop it (the head butting will ruin your hair and the sleepless nights will leave you with bags you can well do without) and allow God, husbands or others to step up to the mark. Yes, it's definitely nerve-wracking and frightening but also extremely liberating to think that it is possible to hand over that responsibility to those to whom it belongs. It's getting out of the boat stuff. And although scary when they won't do it like we want or worse still make key mistakes, trusting God and the lessons learnt by all are worth the effort. We women have to change to see others change. I've watched husband and kids, grow, change and stand tall.

It's the flow-on effect again. Ripples extending to touch one life, yours, then another and another.

If you are one of those women who want change, perhaps you are thinking that I don't know your husband, health, finances, wild child or boss. No, but I do know our God and I do recognise that as you keep hanging on to the responsibility, you'll be continually weighed down and functioning out of your right zone.

As you surrender more of your life and plans to God, allowing others to be themselves without having to fit into your plans, then everyone relaxes, including you. Surrender is hard at first but it works out for the best. This exchange of giving control to God is our gift to Him and others. And it's truly beautiful.

> 'I throw myself on you: you are my God! Hour by hour I place my days in your hand ...'[5]

> ... for it is God's power working unto salvation [for deliverance from eternal death] to everyone who believes with a personal trust and a **confident surrender** ...[6], (bold mine).

For those people who have done you wrong, as you start (and continue) to release and surrender them to God, forgiving and releasing then allows God to change their hearts supernaturally. Miracles in someone on the other side of the world can be changed when you and I surrender our will for His! It's a beautiful exchange. Surrrender for freedom. The Counsellor and Advocate working as only He can with everyone.

Is it time for you to surrender your life to God's control? If you are like me, you might have to do it again once or twice or a thousand more times. But you *can* trust Him. He's had quite a bit of practise dealing with the failings of humanity over the millenniums! He's not surprised and He patiently waits whilst we get it together to finally surrender, depend and lean on Him. It's very freeing.

The next freedom starter is examining what's going on inside our female minds. A lot of thoughts usually. But is it all helpful? I think not.

shut up self and listen

Shelly Beach in her book, The Silent Seduction of Self-Talk, suggests that the conversations in our minds mirror our inner heart and motives that then end up spoken out of our mouth. She suggests that this started in the Garden of Eden, when Satan encouraged Eve to think about and question God's rules.[7]

> *"Did God really say you must not eat any of the fruit... and you won't die ..."*[8]

Sin was born as Adam and Eve decided their future in their thoughts.

This is still how the enemy of our soul operates in my life, and in yours. He is intent on sending questions, doubts and fears into the quiet recesses of our thinking. It's his goal to fill our thoughts with his words so that these become our thoughts, drowning out God's Words.

Within our mind, thoughts and perceptions can then become skewed, producing judgemental, defensive, angry, anxious, jealous, bitter, prideful, critical and rationalising thoughts which in turn produce behaviours that are anything but godly. These started with Satan's lies as subtle thoughts. Thoughts that we believe, thinking them to be our own. They

4 – freedom for starters

only become our own as we accept them.

The average person can have up to 45,000 thoughts per day[9], many of them negative. That's a lot of *boohoo, woe-is-me* and *it's-all-their-fault* thoughts going down right there! All that negative reinforcement is going on round and round in our head. Like a merry-go-round but, unlike the merry-go-round at the theme park which stops, this type of thinking can continue if not dealt with. We worry, get disturbed sleep and try to figure out how to fix things. On and on it goes.

Repeated thinking strengthens those thoughts in our brain so that those thoughts become our reality.

This negative merry-go-round thinking makes a thought a belief.

Psychology suggests that women ruminate more than men (surprise surprise). It's not a mystery then that women also suffer more anxiety and depression. Do we ruminate too much on the negatives, letting worries and problems go round and round in the mind trying to work things out? Believing that we can't help these thoughts and feelings? I fess up. I'm guilty. You too?

Our negative mindsets are *creating* a reality. Here's an example.

If you 'think' that you are a bad public speaker, your mindset would be confirmed if you botched a talk at work. Any future thoughts are now reinforced by the failed talk, strengthening the negative belief. If you had another shot at public speaking, you would probably be worried due to the last experience, '*believing*' you are a bad speaker therefore hampering your ability to prepare well for the next time. This may create a second inadequate performance, therefore setting up ongoing anxiety for any future experiences and so avoidance becomes the only alternative. No more speaking and no more chances to change the belief. It's a self-perpetuating cycle.

There is hope for this mindset problem. We can be proactive about what's going on in our heads in our thinking, to reprogram our brains if we choose.

God has created our brain to reinvent itself, or renew as we are told in Romans, (see 12:2). And science backs this up. Neurogenesis is the forming of new neural tissue in the brain containing neurons and their associated wiring each time there is systematic repetition. It works against us, if the thoughts are negative and repeated again and again (ruminating) becoming our truth or our self-talk. However, if the thoughts are positive, life-giving words from our Creator, these instead can over time become new tissue, new wiring, producing new physical brain physiology. Yes, our thoughts producing reality. Scary stuff and not out of some sci-fi movie but scientifically true.

They *are* then our own. Embedded in a million brain cells. It takes some doing, but new habits can be formed by lots (and lots and lots) of practise. Repeating again and again God's word, the enemy's lies can be rejected and discarded.

It takes a decision to want to think differently. Two middle-aged women I know both suffered horrible incest as young girls at the hands of close relatives. One of these precious ladies found herself pregnant at 11 years old, becoming a mother at 12. Their stories are not easy to hear, but although both have received help over the years to deal with the resulting emotions of such trauma, one has a hopeful positive view of the future while the other woman sees everything as impossible, reliving the past, pain and hurt.

I am not minimising what has been perpetrated against either of these women as children and they, like other hurting people, deserve our love, compassion and help. But like Joyce Meyer, who has suffered an abusive past and by applying God's Word in her life has altered her thinking to receive transformation, we too can also win the battle in our mind.[10]

God says it this way, in 2 Cor. 10:5 AMP;

... and we lead every thought and purpose away captive into the obedience of Christ (the Messiah, the Anointed One)...

With purpose and effort through our experiences we can determine to view our world differently, remembering that although there is evil, there is something (God's hope and strength) in the human spirit that can rise above. Arduous, yes. But absolutely possible as we keep our eyes (and our mind) on the good. And on God. Touché!

Dr Caroline Leaf tweeted;

"Remember, you're not a victim of your biology! You can choose, and every time you choose, you are changing your brain, for better or worse."[11]

As soon as calm leaves you, consider what you have been thinking in the time leading up to the lack of peace. Choose to think differently. You can decide to think instead about what God says about the subject![12]

God talk

Perhaps at times you hear negative voices telling you that you are hopeless and don't measure up. Maybe you are down in the dumps about your husband or health or money or how much you have to do or the state of the world or the economy or who's in government.

What is God saying and how can we distinguish His voice amongst the many voices crowding our headspace?

Thoughts or voices could come from either God, or the enemy of our soul, or our very own nature. If the thoughts or voices don't agree with scripture, then it can't be God as He can't go against His Word.

Okay this is what He's *not* saying. But how can we hear what He is saying? What does His voice sound like?

We live in a busy and noisy world, so it's often difficult to identify the voices. As I type, if I concentrate I can hear the background drone of distant traffic in the quiet leafy suburb where I live. It's easier at night when it's still and quiet to make out other softer sounds such as birds and crickets.

Like the soft sounds in the dead of the night, if we listen in the quiet, we might just hear a God-whisper. Hearing his voice is like hearing the birds if I listen attentively – unnoticed, unless I put the listening antennae up to hear among the bombardment of other noises. It sometimes is a very quiet voice deep inside the spirit, not necessarily audible but something much quieter than a sound. It comes from the direction of the heart.

> ... *a still, small voice.*[13]

To hear Him, it's a good idea to remove distractions (noise) by getting alone, zoning out from life and cares (see section 1 for ways to zone out). To listen from the deepest part of us is where God speaks from. It's a heart thing and it's where peace is. His voice can change us radically from the inside out, as we listen.

> ... *be transformed (changed) by the [entire] renewal of your mind [by its new ideals and its new attitude].*[14]
>
> ... *fix your attention on God. You'll be changed from the inside out ...*[15]
>
> ... *in quietness and confidence shall be your strength ...*[16]

Do you want to be a person who brings fun, laughter, inspiration and joy to people wherever you go? Do you want to bring happiness and freedom with ripples ever-flowing?

To see permanent change will require the hard work of getting quiet and opening up your spiritual listening ear and heart whilst redirecting your thoughts to His words for your life.

Are you prepared to walk on water? He may allow you to sink a little as you surrender control, to depend on Him to bring you through. This boat ride called your life is, after all, His idea!

> *Immediately after this, Jesus insisted that his disciples get back into the boat and cross to the other side of the lake... the disciples were in trouble far away from land, for a strong wind had risen, and they were fighting heavy waves... When the disciples saw him walking on the water, they were terrified... Don't be afraid," he said."Take courage. I am here!*[17]

You can peel away those unnecessary protective personal layers with His help. In the next chapter we will go deeper into behaviours that rob you and me of our freedom. Then, in the final chapter in this section, we will look at what to do to remove the layers and to overcome destructive behaviours.

Look out! You may even start walking on water.

before and after

Catalina was the perfect wife, mother, Christian, book-keeper, daughter, sister. You name it, she was good at it and her life and family ran like clockwork.

Things however changed after the stillbirth of her son. Perfection was now the order of the day as she endeavoured to combat her fear by controlling and shielding her family and her world from pain and disappointment.

I met Catalina during her fourth pregnancy carrying her second boy. Her two girls were the joy of Cat and her husband Tom, but with this pregnancy she was becoming obsessive about perfection. Perfection in all that she did and how they lived. She believed if everything was 'right' there would be no further calamities.

If things didn't go according to her plans she would suffer panic attacks worrying about things that could go wrong with her family and her unborn and this was beginning to affect her family. She knew that something had to give. And she needed to change.

She began to allow God to peel away the protective layers of perfectionism and control that were covering her fears as she started to spiritually grasp that her personal control was an illusion. She was able to step out of the boat into the unknown as she understood that control over the uncontrollable was the result of and a reaction to the pain of her previous loss.

As a strong believer in God and His sovereignty, she slowly began to surrender control and change her thinking that caused her to need to take over. Much of this happened as she practised GMs and discovered God's peace.

Catalina did this hard soul-searching during the latter trimester of her pregnancy. The subsequent drug-free and (miraculous) pain-free birth of Ricky was a joy on many levels. Her freedom and the birth of a bonny, healthy, cheeky little boy, has been a delight for all who have met him.

Catalina today, and every day, releases all of her family's care into God's loving and capable hands.

short and sweet

- As you are healed, you are meant to overflow and share what you have and what you have learnt for spiritual ripple production, Acts 3:6.
- Don't give in to fears of the unknown, step out of your comfort zone to see miracles unfold, John 14:12; 2 Tim. 1:7.
- Healing is a process like peeling an onion. It takes time, commitment and a desire for God's change in our lives, 2 Cor. 3:18.
- God wants us to be spiritually open, to become raw, vulnerable and open to His change to make us who He planned – women of beauty and purpose, Eph. 2:10.
- Giving up control of our lives in total surrender to God might be difficult but the beautiful exchange is receiving God's freedom, Luke 14:33; Rom. 1:16.
- The thousands of merry-go-round negative thoughts we think each day create permanent brain circuitry and habits.
- It's time to change the patterns into positive, God-inspired thoughts instead, Phil. 4:8; Rom. 12:2.
- Choose thinking that lines up with God's Word to change your brain biology, produce real peace and affect change to affect your world and those around you, Phil. 4:7-8.
- To distinguish God's voice takes focussed effort and time in the noisy world we live in, but it will pay off.
- Be persistent, have a listening spirit and make time to be alone to hear, Gal. 6:9; James 4:8.

- Begin to listen to your thoughts discerning if those thoughts are from God, the enemy or the flesh, 2 Cor. 10:5; Rom. 12:2.
- Apply God's Word to the situations you are facing, Ps. 119: 45, 81, 133.

journey journaling

- Find verses that will encourage you to think new thoughts when you want to take up the reins of control. Here are some to start with: Isa. 55:8-12; Luke 14:33; Rom. 1:16, 6:16.

a prayer

Help me Lord to open up those areas in my life that need peeling away. Prepare me to shed unhealthy layers to become the woman of influence that You designed and desire. I give up control and submit to Your will in my life and the lives of those I care about.

Father, I choose to think thoughts based on Your Word to me. I want to accept with joy your ways in my life even when they don't seem to make sense.

Thank You Lord, in Jesus name,

Amen.

5 – freedom stealers

In the last chapter we looked at some starters or first steps towards freedom. Being open to change, surrendering control, being real and hearing God's voice and applying His Word to our life. In this chapter we will examine what you and I are up against within our own flesh that steals our freedom from us, sometimes without realising it. This will set the scene for the final chapter in this section to deal with these issues to get free of them once and for all, so that we can live life to the full, as the Bible suggests[1] in order to overflow freedom and life.

life and bugs

I very much like what technology does. In the same way as I like my car to work, I don't think about or know, (or if the truth be known, really care) what happens under the bonnet or inside the computer. Just get me from point A to B please via my keyboard or in my car! And as technology rapidly advances I continue with much effort (and some struggle) to keep up with those advances, so that I can do the things that I want.

Just like my car, I expect this technology to always work perfectly, synced across my devices and doing its stuff. Always, on time and accurately. Not much to ask, is it? But it doesn't always work as I would like. And I don't often find answers to my questions in the FAQs (frequently asked questions) on websites. Personally, I'd rather have a real live person talk me through my issues. So I put off making the necessary call. But not because these techno wizards aren't helpful. In fact they are extremely patient with this techno dingbat. But it's so long and arduous and it takes a very long time. Sometimes hours and many times, for days. (Apple iCare, once they have my customer number, hand me straight to a supervisor. I guess because I'm special, or maybe because my problems always do take so much work!)

It reminds me of inner healing. It's a job worth doing, but who knows how it works? And it's arduous, even painful. And it takes forever. It's easier therefore to procrastinate. So we put it off and do nothing.

But, like technology, life is not trouble-free. There are problems, glitches, viruses and bugs that upset the balance, throwing everything out, in technology and life. Defining the problem, digging underneath the issues to find reasons, putting in place some strategies to fix them takes time and effort. It may require the wiping away of the old, before restoration can occur.

I've lost count how many times I've had help wiping and restoring my phone but still the thought of removing my data makes me break out in a cold sweat. Restoration is getting everything back to where it was in the beginning, fresh and new and hopefully bug-free after a hardwire wipe first.

When the bugs, in other words the problems of life, get to us, we may function well like my phone. God, like my friendly iCare people, pinpoints bugs, wipes us clean and then restores us, getting us back to new again. He's good at it. In fact, He's the ultimate bug fixer, if we allow Him to do the work in us. Just like technology, we have to firstly work out the problem (bugs in the fruit) then get to the bottom (root) of the issues.

These bugs in our lives affect how we live life and relate to people. Circumstances and things that have happened may have been very unfair and often shape our future, if we allow them to. I've heard it said that our personalties, good and bad, are created up to age 12, then we spend the rest of our lives trying to unlearn the pain.

Psychology has been, and today is, extremely useful for understanding and proposing therapies to help the human condition. But in my experience, working with people who have previously been helped by psychotherapists and secular counsellors, I've seen God often get deeper to the roots of issues with radical transforming power available only to a supernatural God.

roots, fruits and those bugs

In recent years Melbourne suffered a long drought. When it was in full force and water restrictions were severe, I carried buckets to our lemon tree down the back of the garden. I knew the root system needed nutrients only gained by drinking in moisture from the ground via the roots. It would have been a wasted effort in the height of the drought praying for that lemon tree to produce good lemons, whilst ignoring the soil and root system. I had to attend to the roots before any good could come of the fruit.

The Bible talks in both Testaments about good or bad *fruit* resulting from good versus bad roots (see Isaiah 27:6 and Galatians 5:16-23).

Our lives are like my lemon tree. We need to get free from painful past hurts (the roots that produce bad fruit[2]), to produce juicy and healthy lemons or fruit.

It could be time to dig deep to discover the deep issues, so that you can be all you are meant to be. This will probably take a decision to do things differently to how you've managed inner pain in the past. God's way is to uncover the inner issues, triggered by the annoyances and difficulties in life (bugs again). My illustration about technology and not wanting to know how it works is not good enough in our lives. This might look like you saying: I don't need to go there, I'm okay. Even when those close to us are speaking the truth (or yelling to be heard), we don't want to know or get digging.

As God begins to reveal in circumstances and in

relationships that we have issues though, our long-held inbuilt coping mechanisms are threatened so we buck against change. But change is necessary for growth. His way is the best way, no matter how arduous it may seem. He is able to restore us back to be who we are meant to be, full of promise and hope.

He refreshes and restores my life (my self)…[3]

We all start out with history. Our fruit and bugs are often the result of unmet needs, hurts and pain (roots) sustained as we find ways to operate in the midst of our pain. These ways set up specific brain circuitry and physiology, producing habits that seem too hard to break.

I had to unlearn feelings of loneliness and abandonment felt as a child with my often absent sailor dad. This process took time. Your journey of discovery will require, like me, firstly looking at the fruit (actions) affected by bugs (life's challenges) to discover the inner hurts and roots to find freedom. Sometimes if there are many issues, it might be one root and then another and then another. In my healing, feeling alone and abandoned was one diseased root, long-forgotten and buried but causing bitter fruit such as a wild life when life's trials (those bugs) got hard.

If there's bad fruit, there's a bad root.

Jesus works His miracles in digging up roots. Put your faith with your bug-ridden fruit in His hands to let Him begin to uncover and dig deep into your very heart.

the heart of the matter

But our hearts can be a little like the South Pole. A very cold place! In winter months when there is no sunlight at all, it can get as low as minus 58°C! Summer is not much better…it gets as high as a huge minus 25°C. The view is one of cold, stark, lifeless winter desert that stretches in every direction as far as the eye can see. It's a barren wilderness where it's too cold for anything to grow; only the hardiest of visiting sea birds and penguins can survive the harshness of the climate and terrain.

Parts of our hearts are like that, co-existing with otherwise vibrant and happy parts. Past hurts and offences have caused hearts to shut down in sections where life used to grow. And instead now contain cold dark, frozen spots[4]. Often the closed-down heart makes it difficult to be recognised by the owner. It's a protection mechanism operating like a closed window over the pain. Deep-seated and hidden from view, its effect is almost always visible.

God created you and He made a way for you to walk your journey in victory, from a position of power, although it might not seem so in your circumstances. There is a way through and as the Counsellor He wants to guide you to freedom.

What are some of these areas? How do we discover them and open the windows of our hearts? When we look at the roots, we might find cold frozen areas of fear, shame, unforgiveness, anger, guilt and bitterness. They have become covers to protect us from pain but end up becoming sinful actions against God, ourselves or others. The habits that are inevitably produced keep you and me from the freedom that is rightfully ours as children of God. These sins-turned-habits are easier than living right which is harder and requires more effort. But in reality God's way, although sometimes a journey taking some time and effort, is the only way to true liberty.

We may not even recognise the battle is raging within us and around us. Ephesians chapter 6 describes the battle we wage:

5 – freedom stealers

> ... take your stand against the devil's schemes. For our struggle is not against flesh and blood, but against the rulers, against the authorities, against the powers of this dark world and against the spiritual forces of evil in the heavenly realms.[5]

In these next pages we will look at rotten roots and their resulting fruit! Each of them is stealing our freedom. Chances are you'll identify with some before you get to the next chapter on how to deal with them. To be free to be who God purposed from the beginning of time.

fear produces: living-life-afraid fruit

Fear is often the major stumbling block and root cause of many of life's issues. Nations are ruled by it and wars are fought because of it. Hitler feared the Jews and the American civil war was fought fearing slavery law change (who will do the work?) Watch the evening news and see groups rising up against others in fear of people or ways they don't know or want. This is fear in action.

We get so used to living with fears of one kind or another that they become hidden and even unrecognisable as fear. Once the person discovers the fear (easier said than done), dealing with that fear is possible. Facing our personal inner pain takes conscious effort and hard work, which may create discomfort. This is often why it is avoided. After all, who of us likes hard work and pain?

We are bound by fear. Many of us don't make difficult turns into main roads because it's difficult, or drive in the city because of the traffic and parking. We don't speak to so-and-so because we're not good enough, we don't eat certain foods because of our digestion, we can't leave our job because of today's uncertain job market.

The person with a fear of heights will avoid places that

bring that fear on. She is not free, but governed by that fear. Fear of failure may drive him to excel but with often serious consequences to his health and relationships. Fear of man or confrontation may lead to avoidance, rather than facing up to and dealing with difficult situations or relationships. Fear of change may cause her to avoid moving house or changing jobs even when the current environment is uncomfortable. Fear of past confrontation with a relative that has led to bitterness may cause family functions to be avoided.

Henry W. Wright, the senior pastor at Be In Health ministry in Thomaston, Georgia, has built an international ministry helping people find freedom from fears with astounding results. The health benefits and healings are extraordinary.[6]

He suggests that fear operates in a similar way to faith but in the negative as a type of faith in things not hoped for and not yet seen. He tells that he deals with all sorts of fears at his ministry centre, from "phobias, paranoia, delusions, projections, anxiety, panic, panic attacks, phobic realities, agoraphobia, claustrophobia and mother-in-law phobia."[7] He says that fear and other sins against God cause 80% of all disease. Astounding claims, but I have personally seen remarkable improvements in health and healing (osteoporosis, vestibular migraines and MS) in a number of people who have put these theories into practice in their lives.

Whether or not you can accept his teaching, other ministries concur that fear is a sin and should be annihilated from our lives. In the excellent book about living clean in a polluted world, Soul Detox, Craig Groeschel suggests four main fear groups. They are the fear of loss (such as our kids, spouse, finances or control); fear of failure (demands of self or from others, new challenges); fear of rejection (abandonment, causing people-pleasing); and fear of the unknown (the future, ageing, different people groups).[8]

Can you identify with any of those mentioned in the brackets? Chances are that one or some of them hit home with you.

What we believe, even if it's fear, is often a self-fulfilling prophecy. Look at the following scriptures:

> *... according to your faith let it be to you.*[9]

> *For the thing I greatly feared has come upon me, and what I dreaded has happened to me. I am not at ease, nor am I quiet; I have no rest, for trouble comes.*[10]

If you are thinking fearful thoughts, chances are you will have fearful outcomes. If we mentally focus on the danger, biologically, the body goes into danger mode and stress hormones start raging throughout the body causing overload (see chapter 1).

God addresses the issue of fear throughout the Bible with words to overcome anxiety and worry, (see short and sweet at the end of this chapter). Trusting faith in a heavenly and loving Father who has your interest at heart, combats living life afraid. In the reality of moving away from fear, life's journey can become wider, freer and smoother.

unforgiveness produces: strife fruit

Over the years, I have had to do some forgiving. Holding onto unforgiveness actually hurts us sometimes more than those that have done the hurting. And often they are not even aware whilst our insides are being beaten up.

When I've needed to forgive, who needed forgiveness?

Myself, when I've botched things up. And that's pretty often if I'm honest. I had a lot of regret. I could have, should have. You know how it goes.

God, particularly when He hasn't organised my life like I wanted.

And others, when I've taken and held on to offences (not the traffic kind, the ones where people do/say something that gets us all shook up). In fact, I generally need to forgive others on a daily basis. They spoke wrongly, didn't speak, talked too much, took something, left something, came uninvited, didn't invite, didn't agree and on and on it goes. They are the ones in the wrong! Aren't they?

The truth is that when I haven't been able to forgive others easily, I have learnt to make a decision based on what is right as a follower of Christ, (even as I've been screaming inside). Placing myself higher on my judgemental throne until such time as the offender stops or apologises, won't fix a fallen world. What then? God is quite clear. We forgive no matter what. And keep on forgiving, (Matt. 18:22).

If you forgive those who sin against you, your heavenly Father will forgive you.[11]

Forgiving others has nothing to do with what they do or don't do (unfortunately). How good would it be if those who wronged us came and apologised and then never did us wrong again. But that's not the real world. Henry Wright suggests: "When you forgive someone, you are not letting them off the hook but giving them to God, still wiggling *on* the hook. *You* are now off the hook."[12] They might still sin against you but you and I don't have to sin and hold on to unforgiveness. *Their* unforgiveness, or sin, is just that. Theirs. And it's between them and God. Yours and my unforgiveness is our sin. And it's up to us to wipe *our* slate clean by wiping away our sin.

When I find it hard to forgive I have to remember that God has forgiven me and I'm not on the judgement throne. I also find it really helpful to remember what Jesus said from

5 – freedom stealers

the cross. He prayed:

Father, forgive them, for they do not know what they are doing.[13]

Now if you please, the Jewish religious leaders knew exactly what they were doing. They were getting rid of a pesky troublemaker who threatened their power and control. Pontius Pilate knew what he was doing – preventing the chance of trouble from the powerful Jewish quarter and the Roman soldiers were just obeying orders.

The people watching knew what they were doing. They were watching a man who thought He was the Messiah, fall from the pedestal they had only recently placed him on. The disciples and Jesus' followers, who had so genuinely loved and followed Him, knew what they were doing. They were watching, unable to stand up for what they had so recently believed in, and wondering if He had been for real.

Satan and his demons knew what they were doing too. They had orchestrated Judas Iscariot, and the rulers, to get Jesus wiped out.

Jesus, as God, knew it all. But what was really happening? Sin put Him on that cross. and He understood that they didn't know *exactly* what they were doing.

The Father, in the midst of sin was working all things for good (Rom. 8:28). It was the Master plan of plans. In His agony, Jesus was able to forgive them because they didn't know they were crucifying God Himself. They didn't know that in their sin, God's plan would save the world, you and me included. They didn't know, but God did then and God does now.

He knew when you were abused, when you were overlooked for that job. He knew when you were abandoned and when you lost all your money on that deal.

He knew when you lost a child, a parent, a husband before time. He knew and His plan is somehow like the incredible plan at Calvary, an amazing plan for Grace and Love to shine through.

When I have had to forgive betrayal at the hands of my best friends at church or by a family member, it has helped me to remember Jesus' words at the cross. If Jesus can forgive mocking, abuse of a shocking nature, abandonment from His best friends and even for a time separation from the Father, and inconceivable pain and torture, then I should be able to forgive anything. In that light, nothing at all compares, does it?

His forgiveness of the whole world was represented in what was done on the cross, allowed by His faith and trust in the Father's master plan, to resolve the stain of sin from mankind. Your sin and mine.

Your forgiveness does the same. It stops sin in its tracks even when potentially sin could take over. Forgiveness releases a spiritual freedom that nothing else can.

Corrie ten Boom's real-life World War II concentration camp stories are a wonderful example to us all of Christ's power in us to withstand and forgive the unforgivable.[14]

Remember H. Wright suggests that forgiveness doesn't let others off the hook, but leaves them there wiggling on their hooks before God.

Who do you need to forgive to get you off the hook? Let them go, God's got it covered.

pride produces: me-myself-and-I fruit

Lucifer was a beautiful, created angelic being who, unfortunately for us all, wanted to be like God. He desired to be seated on a throne in Heaven above God's throne.[15]

5 – freedom stealers

Take a bow, in comes pride to the human condition – a critical heart issue then and tragically later for all mankind.

Pride – the belief that we are 'owed' because of our importance or value – led Adam and Eve to believe that they had every right to make their own decision about right and wrong. Pride – believing it's okay to eat the forbidden fruit against God's command. Just like Lucifer's pride led him, it produces in you and me selfishness to think we deserve more and better. That we are owed privileges, high position and accolades.

The Bible tells us that we are who and where we are, only by God's infinite grace. Not in our own right. Not by our own making or effort. Only by our faith in God and the atoning death of Jesus are we made blameless and pure and worthy. Pride counteracts that and says "by myself I am worthy".

There's no denying it or getting away from it. Pride breaks the first commandments that say:

> *You must not have any other god but me. You must not make for yourself an idol of any kind ...*[16]

Pride says "I am my god and I deserve first place". Pride says that I am right and everyone else is wrong. Pride focusses on my own self-importance. Just like Lucifer. Ouch!

I was shocked as I began to listen to my self-talk about who I am and what I think I am owed. Particularly in my relationships with others. Some of my full-of-pride self-talk went like this:

> *Who do you think you are saying/doing that to me?*
>
> *Why shouldn't I sit down and enjoy myself like you are? I'm doing all the work. I deserve so much better than to be the slave around here.*
>
> *You think you're so special, anyone can do that! I can*

do that!

Okay God, here's what I want You to do for me today, pretty please.

Look at how they are dressed! I am/look much better than they do. That's because I have great dress sense.

Look at that fat person. They obviously are slack. I'm not like them at all.

Me, myself and I! Pride...and it's ugly! It can often lead to perfectionism. When things or people around me are perfect then I'm happy because they're like me. I'm first and I'm best. Perfect.

Do you relate? Maybe. Our inner thoughts and attitudes reflect this ongoing pride in our heart oftentimes without us even aware of it.

For out of the overflow of his heart his mouth speaks. [17]

Listen to yourself. Just like me, you might get a surprise. Pride pervades within us, our culture, our family and even the church. It's been around a long time and, like fear, it controls our actions from deep inside our spirit.

judgements produce: the blame-game fruit

Christmas was hectic. I had a myriad of things to do. Shopping, catch-ups, cooking and time was moving too quickly. I was waiting for a car to exit a parking spot and someone else snuck in and drove right in there. I wanted to scream and yell and tell them a thing or two (or more not to be admitted to here).

In my opinion (by the look of the exiting driver), that pusher-inner was definitely in the wrong. I was there first and that's the unwritten rule, first there, gets the park. Agreed?

I might label them selfish, pushy and greedy, or other

colourful endearments (not) that came to mind on that day. But the truth is that I didn't have a clue what that driver was up against that day. Maybe he or she was just being ignorant and selfish or maybe, just maybe, they had an urgent need for a park, so getting that park any-which-way was for them justifiable. After all is said and done, that spot did *not* belong to me, with my name on it, just because I happened along first. (Much!)

Not that I'm judging them at all. Lol! Well maybe a little.

As human beings we tend to judge others by their actions but judge ourselves by our intentions. Read that again? We can only know our inner thoughts and not other people's. So we often judge without knowing the full details.

Let me describe this visually so that it's easier to understand it. We see right and wrong as opposites so on a continuum, right and good are at one end with wrong and bad at the opposite end.

Right & Good *Wrong & Bad*

When people don't measure up to our expectations, like taking my car park, we see them as wrong or bad or in the black according to our measurement of right. We, of course, are right or good and as white as snow, because we know our heart.

Many times we and the other side are not completely right or wrong but somewhere in-between as slightly imperfect sinners.[18] And we each view any situation from completely different angles or perspectives. Each with our own hurts, pain and situations, surviving in life.

So we all need a little bit (or a lot) of grace for the actions and predicaments that others find themselves in, even if their circumstances stem from bad choices. Remember when you mucked up last? I do (well with a bit of help from my honest spouse).

In reality we are all somewhere along that continuum. Neither white nor black. Right or wrong. We're all just a shade of grey – somewhere in the middle and there's a whole heap of grey between black and white. So don't judge!

Can you remember when someone took your car park, or when your husband snapped without reason, or when the neighbours let their dog bark at night or when that person abused you, or your beloved daughter or son swore and left the home … the list goes on. There are many shades of grey.

Joyce Meyer often says on her programs that hurting people hurt people. Even the abuser oftentimes was the abused at one time. They too deserve our compassion, not our blame.

Maybe God wants you and me, no matter how unfair our past, to look at ourselves first. Perhaps there's something in us that we are blind to.

> … Why do you see the splinter that's in your brother's or sister's eye, but don't notice the log in your own eye? How can you say to your brother or sister, 'Let me take the splinter out of your eye, when there's a log in your eye?[19]

Your freedom begins in you. And my freedom begins in me. You and I are just not as perfect as we would like to think we are. All of us are being perfected by a God who knows and loves us anyway.

envy and idols produces:
I want more fruit

I am competitive by nature. This has meant that I have had to work hard to realise my goals and ambitions. To win, to be the best, to go after my dreams. All my life I studied hard, played hard, worked hard to achieve and keep achieving. This has given me a reputation for reliability and getting things done on time and to a high standard. Good attributes to have. Except when these come at a personal cost. Continual striving is hard to maintain and produces persistent stress.

When God showed me that I was always looking at others, comparing myself with how they spoke, taught, preached and acted in every way, I suddenly saw this wasn't such a good thing. The root was envy. Coveting what others had or could do; putting others on a pedestal as an idol; and comparing myself with their skills and talents... born from a fear of rejection.

As women, we're pretty good at this type of ugliness. Wanting nice homes, (clean of course with everything in place), well-behaved children, living in the best suburb, the best job, husband, latest car, best schools/education for the kids, knowing people in high places, designer clothes, hairstyle and the list continues. It comes down to wanting what others have or what others can do. These 'things' we reason will help us to feel accomplished, becoming happier and fulfilled. Craig Groeschel suggests:

> *"When our moods and emotional needs depend on acquiring more possessions, more money, more toys, then we're in for a toxic shock when we find our hands full and our hearts empty."*[20]

Many girls seem to struggle with envy. It could look like

self-esteem issues in trying to measure up; people pleasing (comparing what we want to do with what others expect us to do); striving, boasting in what we have or what our kids have done; working two/three jobs to have the latest mod cons; aiming for endless promotions to be noticed as having arrived. Fit into any of these? You may identify with at least one.

The last of the Ten Commandments that God gave to Moses on Mt Sinai was regarding this very issue.

> *Neither shall you covet your neighbour's wife, nor desire your neighbour's house, his field, his manservant or his maidservant, his ox or his donkey, or anything that is your neighbour's.*[21]

How many of your actions, of my actions, are based on envy? Wanting what others have? What does this cause in our lives?

> *And what do you benefit if you gain the whole world but lose your own soul? Is anything worth more than your soul?*[22]

These 'things' trick us into believing that we will have significance if we achieve or own them. But this is so far from the truth. The truth is that only God fulfils us and completes us. He created us unique and will provide what we need to be whole and live with purpose. He designed you and me to be the people we are with the skill set that we own, living within the means we are capable of, rather than in our lack, looking at others and comparing. Comparing is ugly.

I will talk on gratitude some more in chapter 7. But for now, switch your thinking about what others are doing. That's their race, not for you to run. You run *yours* in *your* unique way and be about *His* ways.

self pity produces: poor-me fruit

Have you asked yourself these? Or felt that? I have. Too many times. It leads to a whining spirit that isn't pretty. The complaining in the head leads to whining out of the mouth. Things like, no-one ever helps me in the kitchen; it's always muggins mum who has to take the responsibility; why has my health always been bad, nothing is fair! I needed a reality check!

It came one day when I was complaining to God about the mess in my kitchen and how I was once again the one cleaning up after others. I felt Him whisper a question for me to think about. Would I rather have a kitchen in Africa with a cooking fire (that I have to light), a few bowls and some cutlery and be working (and walking) on a dirt floor. Whoops, I was stopped in my tracks.

This *poor me* attitude I realised had been with me for much of my life. The revelation that had some ugly fruit, hit me right between the eyes. And in my heart. Like a tonne of bricks. It's called self-pity. Having countless pity parties on a daily basis. This thinking had made me act ugly. It was keeping me from God's best because I wasn't grateful for what He had done and what I had.

I made a decision that day. Instead of complaining, I began to say, thank you God for my kitchen, my home, the food in my cupboard and appliances to cook with. Thank you, thank you, thank you Lord.

having gratitude can change the course of our lives

Two girls I ministered to were similar in their backgrounds and situations. They had been involved with guys in long-term relationships that hadn't worked out. They found themselves without partner prospects in their late 30s, devastated and somewhat desperate. Their body clocks were ticking and the available time to start families was reducing rapidly with each passing year. This can be devastating to many women who desire to have a family.

As women we all at times find ourselves in difficult situations, perhaps not of our own making. But as the verse says, a strong spirit can overcome.

> *The strong spirit of a man sustains him in bodily pain or trouble, but a weak and broken spirit who can raise up or bear?*[23]

God never said life would be easy but He did say He wouldn't leave us.[24] He means for us to rise above our circumstances no matter how challenging. After all, He has allowed the difficulty in our lives. And most probably for a specific purpose or work that He wants to do in us. We are to look upwards instead of focussing on the difficulty around us. And as we look up, He does miracles *in us* that enable miracles *around us*.

What happened to these girls without partners? Both are now in their early 40s. One is still single and still desperate to find her spouse (she reflects this). The other, as she got older and marriage looked more impossible, chose to get closer to God. She replaced the 'poor me' thoughts in her head with what the Bible says about godly counsel. She didn't give up on church or God or herself. She began to be grateful for her life and the blessings that she did have. And as she gave up her need for a man to complete her, allowing God to be that for her, guess what? Yes. Mr Right came along. As I write this, I'm looking forward to attending her wedding ceremony tomorrow. How wonderful God is.

Often the death of our dreams can become a stimulus

for change, growth and miracles. From death to life! Like all freedom stealers, if we remain in our misery, dwelling on unfairness and lack, breakthrough is elusive. For me, recognising the root of self-pity from my childhood loneliness helped me see, to start getting free. And for the other girl looking for her life partner, she has been unable or unwilling to investigate her roots, instead still trying to fix the fruit by still desperately searching for the man of her dreams.

I am giving up on feeling sorry for myself because I have to clean up the crumbs all the time in the kitchen. I'm going to be grateful for my blessings, kitchen, health, family and ministry. In short, my life. How much grace we have been given by our God.

How about you?

You and I have been created to fulfil a magnificent purpose in order to create ever-extending ripples of influence.

In the meantime, each of us is on a journey and a work in progress as we continue to unearth, dig up and discard.

In the next chapter, I will list specific strategies to deal with the freedom stealers in your life that might have been unearthed in this chapter. You can have healthy and beautifully sweet-tasting fruit. Delivery straight to your door.

before and after

Myra (a successful accountant in her early 30s) and her boyfriend planned to marry. They bought a house and moved in together. Two years later after battling unsuccessfully to make the relationship work, he moved out and she was left with the mortgage and a broken heart.

Months later she was still emotionally wounded, not knowing how to be healed. She was a new believer, discovering God's love through a new relationship with Jesus but was still plagued by anguish, failure, thoughts of her ex-partner and a fear of relationships. What was she up against?

Myra was in a battle of sorts, a spiritual one. As a new Christian she knew God's love and was destined for Heaven but still needed some answers for her pain. Like Myra, we are all in a battle. It may not look like Myra's but there's an opponent that is out to get us in whatever area we are weakest. The chink in our armour.

Myra dug deep inside herself to discover some of the roots to her issues, recognising that from childhood she had believed the lies told to her that she was useless, stupid and of little value. The result? Self-pity, low self-esteem, unforgiveness, fear and a deep-held belief that as a bad person, she didn't deserve love. Rotten fruit. And untrue.

She continued to search deep, receiving revelations that God indeed loves her and has a plan for her life. She forgave herself for not being perfect, forgave her fiancé and her family.

Myra continues to hand over her fears to God, forgives and is growing stronger (and freer) as she depends more and more on Him.

Recently, she began a new relationship with a young, caring Christian man. And she is glowing! *And* also overflowing.

short and sweet

- Problems and circumstances in life are a lot like annoying bugs in our technological world. Wiping the old is sometimes required to release the new, Rom. 5:3.
- We all carry unnecessary stuff from our past: unmet needs, hurts and pain.
- The fruit of our lives is the result of healthy or diseased *roots*, Deut. 29:18; Heb. 12:15.
- Fear, shame, unforgiveness, anger, guilt and bitterness come from hurts in our hearts, Deut. 29:18-19.
- God is our helper, counsellor and advocate in our healing, John 14:16.
- One of the major root issues producing bad fruit from bugs in our lives is fear, 2 Tim. 1:7; Heb. 11:1, 3.
- We can use scriptures to boost faith instead of fear, Matt. 9:29; Matt. 21:21; Rom. 1:17, 10:17, 12:3; Heb. 10:23, 38, 11:1,3,6; Ps. 23:4.
- Trust God, Job 13:15; Ps. 37:3-5; Prov. 3:5-6.
- Forgiveness of others, God and ourselves gets us off the hook with them still wiggling on the hook, Neh. 9:17; Matt. 6:14, 18:22.
- Another of the major root issues producing baggage in our lives is pride begun in the garden, Gen. 3:1-6; Prov. 16:18; 8:13.
- Pride can often be discovered by listening to our inner self-talk, Prov. 29:23.
- Don't judge others. We are not always either right or wrong, but all slightly imperfect, Rom. 3:23.

- It's up to us to examine ourselves rather than pointing out and judging the flaws of others, Matt. 7:3-5.
- Wanting what others have is envy or coveting, Ex. 20:17.
- Putting others on a pedestal is idol worship, Jer. 13:27.
- Be grateful, Ps. 63:5-8; 1 Cor. 8:3.
- Feeling sorry for yourself, complaining, self-pity is linked to envy (coveting) and pride. Be grateful instead, Phil. 4:11.

journey journaling

- Can you relate to any of these resulting fruits? Being fearful, judgemental, defensive, angry, anxious, jealous, bitter, prideful, critical of others?
- Do you need to forgive yourself or God? Share your thoughts with God and perhaps a trusted friend.

a prayer

Jesus, help me to discover and remove any root issues in my life that cause me to sin. Forgive me for the sins of fear, unforgiveness, envy and (others).

I forgive _____

(those that have hurt me in any way)

and I release them from my judgements, as they didn't know what they were doing. Thank you Lord,

Amen.

6 – seize your freedom

In the previous chapter we looked at some of the fruit that might be evident in your life that is keeping you from your best. These include fear, unforgiveness, shame, guilt, anger, bitterness, pride, judgements, idol worship and self-pity. What a depressing list! Particularly if you identify with several of them. However, take heart, although they may seem insurmountable problems to overcome, by identifying them, the first major step to freedom has been made.

Getting rid of unhealthy fruit and then growing healthy fruit will take spiritual digging that requires courage and fortitude. By doing this God's way, accessing His power, love and grace, seizing your freedom is possible and within reach.

So are you ready for some change? In this chapter you will discover practical strategies to do just that and as a result be a positive influence in your world. Prepare to walk on waves.

love, happiness and fruit

Every person now and throughout history has a desire to be happy. Loving and being loved is a prerequisite to happiness. Our sense of worth depends on love, which as a consequence brings contentment and joy in life. Although happiness can also be experienced alone on a beautiful day or after a satisfying achievement, knowing love in our life brings fulfilment as we were created to be in relationship with God and others.

Some of your happiest memories may have been your wedding day, the birth of your children, receiving a gift from a friend, getting the desired role in a great company or moving into your new family home.

So how do we find love and subsequently happiness? Science is discovering what the Bible has told us for centuries. Acts such as generosity, kindness, love and gratitude help us to feel loved and happy.[1]

Unfortunately, many of us try to find happiness in the wrong places, with the wrong people and for the wrong reasons. A young man I know who has Asperger's Syndrome (a form of autism, causing communicative and interactive social challenges[2]) moved in the wrong crowd looking for a sense of belonging. These 'friends' took him to nightclubs, spent his single mother's hard-earned savings by getting into a joint bank account and maxed out his credit card. There was so much suffering as a result of his search for love and happiness.

Only God has the answer to our continual search. As you read the following verses, replace the word *love* and *it* with God because the Bible tells us that *He is love*[3]. And this is who and what is available for every one.

> *Love is patient and kind. Love is not jealous or boastful or proud or rude. It does not demand its own way. It is not irritable, and it keeps no record of being wronged. It does not rejoice about injustice but rejoices whenever the truth wins out. Love never gives up, never loses faith, is always hopeful, and endures through every circumstance.*[4]

When we meet Him (Love) for the first time, we understand immediately that we have come home and are finally, truly and completely loved. He sent His precious Son to reconcile our relationship with Him that was severed in the garden of Eden by sin.[5] Happiness and love must therefore spill out from us as His love flows in us. What an exchange. Love for sin.

The love journey however is another matter. It takes some perseverance to commit and be available for His direction and use, even though we are blessed in the process. Those freedom stealers discussed in the last chapter such as fear, pride and the rest can only be cancelled out through the outworking of His perfect love in us.

> *There is no fear in love [dread does not exist], but full-grown (complete, perfect) love turns fear out of doors and expels every trace of terror!*[6]

Simple and easy it should be, but also difficult. You see, we are so used to doing things our own way. But with diligence, perseverance and a little (or a lot) of surrendering, amazing fruit is produced.

> *... the fruit of the [Holy] Spirit [the work which His presence within accomplishes] is love, joy (gladness), peace, patience (an even temper, forbearance), kindness, goodness (benevolence), faithfulness, gentleness (meekness, humility), self-control (self-restraint, continence).*[7]

God's love working *in* and through us. What can *we do* to access this?

We need a heart attitude of gratitude to God, maybe some prayer and fasting (yes, some people can go without food). And then uncovering deeply held belief systems that are causing diseased roots. As these are finally handed over to God we receive in return freeing revelations.

an attitude of gratitude

How is your attitude looking right now? Who has upset you? Who is in the wrong?

Before you can have an attitude of gratitude, it's a good idea to get some things off your chest. Journaling is a great way to do that. Those things that are decidedly negative in your thoughts and attitude. You probably know them but ask God for some insight into any blind spots as you prayerfully journal. They might include people or things that upset you or make your blood boil. Here are a few of mine. (You might look like an angel after reading mine. Don't judge me, okay?)

Self-pity about being muggins-mum of the kitchen; worry about sleep and the lack of it; worry about lack of time all the time; wrinkles; money; flabby arms (terrible right?); not being recognised for the truly brilliant speaker that I am (ha ha horrible, I warned you). The list goes on. You probably get the picture. I don't want you to have any more illusions of me ruined, so I'll stop here.

Hey I'm being honest! Now it's your turn. (I'm off the hook!) Write them down, offer them up to God and His Divine Sovereignty then draw a line in the sand (the journal), beginning from today, to do things differently. To begin, write a list of the amazing things to be thankful for plus the miraculous times God has come through for you.

Taken from my journal, here are some of the things that I'm grateful to God for:

Owning a reliable car that works when I turn the key; living in a free Australia; that my children are well and love God (it wasn't always this way); having a faithful and supportive husband; my God-given calling making a difference in women's lives. And some of the miracles I've seen: seeing God work a miracle in C's dad when we prayed for him; M's transplant success after praying for renewed emotional health; my husband hearing from God when he didn't always hear me (try this, it's not a bad prayer – beats nagging); watching S's healing from MS at Be In Health[8] USA–2013; healing our son; continued healing in my body from a painful bulging disc.

As I add to and read over my gratitude journal each morning, it's easier to forget the problems that I face because I remember that I am incredibly blessed by God.

You could do this to direct your thoughts towards happy and grateful situations and memories and you'll be surprised to find that your attitude changes as a result. Feel-good hormones can be produced that can boost your immune system, making you feel better and look better (bye bye wrinkle-producing frowns). You'll actually be better off.

If on the other hand I think about all those things that are going wrong (there's a zillion right?...like wrinkles, oh yes!... did I mention my recent wrinkle-watching phobia?) and I think about them often enough and for too long I actually feel worse and see more of those little critters.

Same goes for you. Those problems that are affecting you at this time will seem worse and as God says in Job 3:25 NLT ... *What I dreaded has come true*. In other words those things might just happen that way if you don't let them go.

Hey, I'm turning over a new leaf. I'm going to be glad that I've got wrinkles, because I'm still here, alive and growing in God. That's going in my gratitude journal tonight.

Sometimes when I need an attitudinal makeover, *going without* seems to help me cleanse the soul. Let's talk about fasting, and don't you run away now! It might not be quite as bad as you imagine and you might even get excited.

prayer and fasting? no way!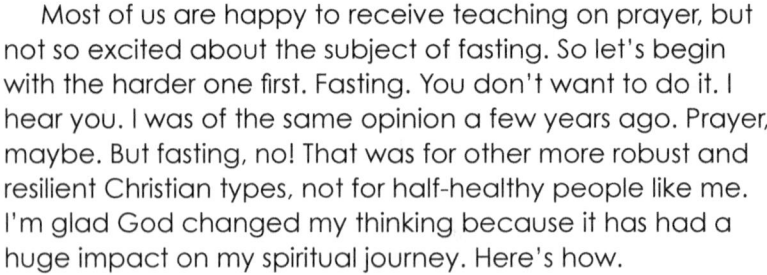

Most of us are happy to receive teaching on prayer, but not so excited about the subject of fasting. So let's begin with the harder one first. Fasting. You don't want to do it. I hear you. I was of the same opinion a few years ago. Prayer, maybe. But fasting, no! That was for other more robust and resilient Christian types, not for half-healthy people like me. I'm glad God changed my thinking because it has had a huge impact on my spiritual journey. Here's how.

Our church started to pray and fast together and I wanted to be a part of it. I knew I could pray on my own and in the combined prayer meetings but I wanted more. I didn't think that I could stop eating for health reasons (I was a migraine sufferer at the time), so I asked God what could I do? (Always a good idea to ask God, right?)

I sensed in my spirit the answer was to remove white sugar from my diet for the fast period. Although a challenge, I felt I could probably do it successfully. So for the next 21 days of the church fast, I ate no white sugar. This meant checking labels and removing some (not all) desserts and I got through still smiling and in one piece. But importantly, I discovered a new spiritual world open up. I found that I heard God's voice during this time more clearly than in my entire Christian journey. But after the fast was over I sensed that the volume switch to God's voice had been turned off.

I missed Him. And His voice. And I wanted Him back. What now? Back to God to check with Him (still a good idea). This time, I felt my answer was to simply keep going. I'd heard about great faith preachers who lived a lifestyle of fasting that sounded interesting. Maybe like them, I could have the God-speak volume on, all the time. So I continued the same sugar-free fast.

Fasting has been transforming for my prayer life, the closeness I feel to God and for my ministry and life directions. Although over the years, the type of fasting has periodically changed from the first fast to weekday-only sugar fasts, or dessert or snack fasts, or lunchtime fasts. I heard and God has directed my different fasts for many years. Lunch, sweets, snacks, sugar. For me fasting is not about rules and regulations (let's not get too weird here) but about being close to my God. In my experience, the more we do *for* God, the more we *need* God and His voice. Fasting makes that possible.

There's even more good news about fasting. Reducing kilojoule intake significantly for two non-consecutive days each week, is now suggested by medical professionals as a healthier alternative to dieting. Others benefits of this routine include cleansing the body from toxins which could result in improving health and even longevity.[9] So not only do we give our spiritual muscles a workout, but we also get healthy in the process! Don't you just love it when science proves God's ways are best?

Why do I mention fasting right now? To explain that fasting included in a person's life (*even yours!*) can provide a solid foundation for tremendous growth. If you feel that God is leading you in this, not as a religious requirement but as an added bonus, like me and many others, you too may experience its benefits.

So what is a fast? There are different types. A full fast is one that includes eating little or no food, but drinking fluids for one or more days (not for the faint-hearted). A Daniel fast,[10] as described in the Bible, is one where the only food eaten is limited to fruits and vegetables with fluids. A partial fast (what I do) means to reduce your meal size or quantity of meals in a day or to remove certain things from your diet or life. Some people give up chocolate, junk food, TV, computer games, desserts or fizzy drinks. Whatever you do, it needs to be okay with the doctor, your spiritual oversight and with God.

Fasting isn't necessarily about physical hunger, but about the heart attitude in sacrificing something that you like or enjoy, for God. He honours your attitude of submission, surrender and obedience. And the blessings that come as a result are well worth the pain of going without.

A mentor friend posted the following in response to my blog on fasting:[11]

> " ... how strong the mind is and learning how to discipline it regarding things I desire, or enjoy ... [it's about] putting down the hunger, or desire to indulge myself when there were more important things to be done ... as an exercise of my will ... I committed myself to fast from the shops and books, ... and asked for His help as I walked through these days ... as a result I grew more hungry for God and eternal values ... [and] to feed the part of me that is eternal to get more related to my Creator."

Beautiful isn't it? You can have this too. You can do it!

Let's talk about praying now. First up, just like communicating with those we care about is important to maintaining a healthy relationship, prayer is communicating with God and in terms of our relationship with Him, is an essential ingredient. If you haven't done much of that before, there's no need to feel guilty or condemned and there's no time like the present to start! A good reason to get motivated is that God longs to spend time with you. You are His special child and He loves you just like we love our own kids. And it's a very special feeling when they want to spend time with us and it's the same with our Heavenly Father.

To achieve a prayer time, it might work for you to get out of bed early to have some quiet time with God. Perhaps a prayer walk during the day or sitting quietly in the evening when the kids are in bed might be better alternatives for you in your current life season. Whatever you choose, you'll get more out of the 15minutes or hour with God than any other way you could spend your valuable time.

Many people don't know what to do in their quiet time. If you don't know what to say, talk with God as you would a best friend that you would tell how you feel about the things/people in your life. Even though He knows all about you, it's releasing for us to download our heart to Him and have His Holy Spirit flow into those private inner 'soft spots'.

As well as downloading, it's good to pray specific prayers for your health, finances and relationships; needs for friends, family, your church, the church, the lost, plus all those other things that need change in our world. To achieve all of those you would need a long list but instead you could use a prayer pattern or template. There are great ones that have been devised (Google can help). You could choose from the Lord's Prayer,[12] or Dr Yongi Cho's Tabernacle Prayer[13] or praying according to acronyms like A.C.T.S., which stands for adoration, confession, thanksgiving and supplication (asking).

Or attempt your own by praying scripture in the first person, such as the Psalms (try 139, 91, and 23). I often use Ephesians 6:10-18 to pray if there is difficulty in my life as I pray and fight spiritual battles using God's armour.

If you can it's great to learn verses that mean a lot to you and pray them over your life and the lives of family and friends. I have prayed Jeremiah 29:11 in my early morning prayer time for my son for more than seven years and I have seen great changes in his life as a result.

> *For I know the plans I have for you,' declares the LORD, 'plans to prosper you and not to harm you, plans to give you hope and a future.*[14]

In whatever way you decide to pray, let your main reason for praying be to seek a deeper relationship with God. Out of that you will find hope for any struggle you might face plus so much more.

So I hope that prayer and fasting *is* for you and that you have learnt that it's not impossible but extremely doable. It will prepare you by building your spiritual strength ready for whatever comes your way and in the case of this chapter, for some hard work to uncover any roots affecting your freedom. Remember to check with your medical professionals, pastoral leadership and God's direction. Then go for it. I trust that you will find it as miraculous as I have.

Remember to surrender, adopt an attitude of gratitude and let's begin to dig up some dirt.

In preparation for inner healing that I cover in the following pages, I strongly recommend that you have support from a trusted pastor or prayer minister experienced in inner healing. Do not attempt this process, particularly if you are a new Christian or a person unused to this type of ministry, without some counsel.

feeling to healing

First we need to talk about sin.

When our children were small and acting up, my husband and I didn't love them any less for their bad behaviour. We attempted to love unconditionally, to bless them often and in any way we could, but when required we handed out consequences for bad behaviour. We were not always perfect parents and in many ways when I look back, we could have done a better job of it. You may or may not have had parents who loved you as well as we all deserve. Unconditionally.

Sometimes we learn from a young age to behave in a certain way or manner to gain approval or acceptance. This may have led to needing fame, assets, money or education to make you feel significant and worthy. This is counterfeit, not truth. God's truth says you are loved and acceptable as you are. You may believe that you are not worthy of God's love, grace and mercy. He made you and by your faith in God you are made right in Him.

... We are made right with God by placing our faith in

Jesus Christ. And this is true for everyone who believes, no matter who we are.[15]

But we are a product of a fallen world and often imperfect early nurturing results in wrong beliefs affecting how we act, believing lies rather than truth. The resulting fruit is ungodly and even when we want to change it is difficult. To see change in our fruit does require changing the deeply believed, ingrained lies. Craig Groeschel in his excellent book, *Soul Detox*, puts it like this:

> "When we truly change what we believe, we'll gladly change how we behave."[16]

In John 8, Jesus protected a woman caught in adultery from being stoned to death by the religious Jews. He told the crowd to throw the first stone if they were free of sin, but no one did. With His loving grace He made a strong point that sin is in people's lives and that He has freedom available. Like her, once sin is discovered He wants us to take responsibility to be rid of it.

... from now on sin no more ...[17]

A good sin illustration is described well in a story of a young boy who wanted to watch a movie that his mother felt was not appropriate as it wasn't honouring to God. He told his mum, it's got just a *little bit* of bad stuff but it's really not too bad. To teach him to make wise decisions and to describe sin's spread, she made him his favourite biscuits with just a *little bit* of dog manure in them, to explain that just a little sin can be a little too much.[18] That's true isn't it? A little bit of manure in a biscuit will have a whole lot of taste! A small amount of sin in us can be causing us bigger problems with wide-reaching consequences.

We often don't recognise where our sinful behaviour starts or why we do what we do. The way that I am going to suggest that we dig up some dirt to uncover any problem-causing roots, is to revisit any intense emotional feelings experienced during a negative event that has affected you (bad fruit). As a result you may have felt unable to function as normal. These initial intense feelings will serve as directional arrows leading to the deep soul issues (roots). These are often formed lies (rather than spiritual truths expressed and taught in the Bible) developed as protective mechanisms against previous hurts. These lies lead to our sin. Unearthing these begins the process of discovery and healing.

The feelings expressed or internally repressed, may tell a lot about us. Sometimes we might be completely blind to the reasons we act or feel certain ways. To discover these lies, we can gain insight by intense feelings asking **why** questions to get to the bottom of the belief system. It's a bit like digging the soil around the root system of our unhealthy tree to discover any disease there.

Remember a time when you felt strongly conflicted and perhaps on an emotional roller-coaster. Journal the event that triggered the feelings, being gentle with yourself as this may be difficult. We can become very skilled at masking our feelings, pushing them deep down, which when brought to the surface are painful.

Here's some questions that might help those feelings get out and then below that a list of feelings that you might identify with.

- What are you most afraid of?
- What is missing? Do you feel empty? What are you filling up on or self-medicating with (e.g. food, shopping, pornography, prescription medication etc)?
- What feelings do you avoid?
- Are you afraid of rejection? Being labelled

inadequate? That others might control you? Of failing?

- Do you hold a grudge? Seek revenge? Does anger lead you to negative statements?

Circle those feelings below that best describe how you felt at a time of intense emotion after upsetting events.

Then select the most intense feeling right now. This will be your first feeling to work through to uncover a lie. The others that you circle might be best left for another time. (Remember to get help if you need it.)

feelings chart [19]

Anxious: uneasy, embarrassed, frustrated, nauseated, ashamed, nervous, restless, worried, stressed;

Afraid: scared, anxious, apprehensive, boxed in, burdened, confused, distressed, fearful, frightened, guarded, hard-pressed, overwhelmed, panicky, paralysed, tense, terrified, worried, insecure;

Traumatized: shocked, disturbed, injured, damaged;

Angry: annoyed, controlled, manipulated, furious, grouchy, grumpy, irritated, provoked, frustrated;

Low Energy: beaten down, exhausted, tired, weak, listless, depressed, detached, withdrawn, indifferent, apathetic;

Alone: avoidant, lonely, abandoned, deserted, forlorn, isolated, cut off, detached;

Sad: unhappy, crushed, dejected, depressed, desperate, despondent, grieved, heartbroken, heavy, weepy;

Betrayed: deceived, fooled, duped, tricked;

Confused: baffled, perplexed, mystified, bewildered;

Ashamed: guilty, mortified, humiliated, embarrassed,

exposed.

why, why, why to uncover the lie

Once you've isolated your main painful feeling/s this next step should help you uncover the diseased root – the believed lie.

Ideally, this should be a prayerful process asking the Holy Spirit for guidance during that time. I suggest extended quiet uninterrupted time wherever possible. Sometimes it may take several sessions so be patient with yourself and the time it takes.

Ask yourself **why** you **feel** a certain way and continue asking until you uncover a 'root' **belief**.

For example, one might feel angry towards a spouse who has spoken unkind words, so the angry person would select the word 'angry' from the list and ask 'why do I feel so angry?' The answer that comes to mind might be 'because it's unfair'. Next would be, 'why do I feel this is unfair? The answer could be, 'because it makes me feel bad'. 'Why does it/this person make you feel bad?' The answer, 'because I feel inferior'. More whys could lead to the belief that 'I am worthless' or 'I'm a failure' or 'I don't measure up' or 'I'm no good'. All lies.

I believed lies for most of my life. Associated with feeling abandoned, this created in me the lie that **I am unlovable** and **unworthy** of love. These were discovered by digging down via the emotional hotspots (feelings) in my relationship with my husband. The emotions of feeling hurt and unloved by him were actually my own bad fruit resulting from my deep inner beliefs, formed from early and long-forgotten memories.

To test these inner beliefs as being truth or lies we hold

them up to scripture. If they don't agree, they're not truth. For my believed lies, Eph. 3:18-19 tells me how enormous God's love is for me and Ps. 139:17-18 tells me how precious I am to Him and that He thinks about me all the time. This is truth. Therefore what I have believed are lies.

Digging deep using why, why, why until there is a solid 'root' or lie which describes you as a person[20] is revisiting emotional pain, potentially very uncomfortable, even agonising. The reason for this is that from an early age, we probably have learnt to 'stuff' wounded feelings.

During this pain and discovery, ask for help and expect God's amazing love, acceptance and grace, through His Holy Spirit before you move on. There is no time limit or condemnation in this process.[21]

four Rs to freedom

Patrick had some problems that had contributed to the breakdown of his marriage. He battled addictions and was passive in his relationships with others. He had several ministry sessions using the questioning techniques of asking why again and again until he remembered that as a child he had been told he would never amount to anything. He grew up to believe the lie that he was **useless**.

The result? Internal emotional pain that caused him to escape (fruit) through addictive behaviour (pornography and drinking) zoning out (more fruit) to block the pain. He was passive (and more) with his wife and children, believing he couldn't make good decisions.

In the ministry sessions he began by taking personal *responsibility* rather than blaming his circumstances on others or God. The lie was uncovered, and he *repented* for believing it, then *rejected* it and asked to receive a *revelation* of truth from God. He glimpsed an inner visual picture of God's hand helping him stand up in a boat amidst a stormy sea as he stepped out on to the water in faith. This brought truth, peace and assurance about his abilities to succeed in difficulty. It was a powerful picture, from the Bible account of Peter's walk on the water[22] that gave him a new confidence and assurance. He is letting go of the addictions and is feeling positive and optimistic about himself and his future.

There are four words to help you get free today and to remember for the future to unearth any hidden lies. They are responsibility, repent, reject and revelation.

responsibility

Our response to discomfort in our lives can be to run from it, deny it or face it head-on and deal with it. If a pattern continues where friends or family keep telling us the same thing, then the problems could be ours to face. Then our response needs to be 'this is my deal, I'm taking *responsibility* for fixing it'.

> ... let us cleanse ourselves from everything that can defile our body or spirit. And let us work toward complete holiness ... the pain caused you to repent and change your ways.[23]

If you have identified any deep issues or sins in your life, it is the first step to be free of pain. Just like the adulterous woman, Jesus required her and us to make the decision to change.[24]

Many of the *little sins* or root issues in people's lives are based on a fear, which governs their behaviour. (See the previous chapter for more about fear.)

You may be able relate to or recognise some in your life,

in your immediate family or extended family. You can take responsibility for anything that you see in yourself or even other family members to begin to see spiritual healing. Those sins in family members could be generational sins passed down and are mentioned as iniquities in the Old Testament (see Exodus 20).

Here's a list of sins and the resulting fruit or ways we act outside of God.

Fear: anxiety, worry, stress, burnout, sleeplessness;

Accusations: unforgiveness, self-pity, martyrdom, idol worship of self, pride, attention seeking, manipulation, taking offence, critical spirit, unbelief, judgements, guilt, suspicion, rebellion, shame, gossip;

Unforgiveness: bitterness, resentment;

Covetousness: envy, jealousy, competition, rivalry, control, stealing;

Rejection: abandonment, insecurity, isolation and loneliness, drivenness, legalism, religious legalism, approval seeking, hopelessness.

repent

The next R-word is to *repent*, asking for forgiveness for believing lies instead of God's truth. The truth is that you are made in His image,[25] are a new creation[26] and eternally loved[27]. Anything less than this is not His truth for you and your life. We need His help to stop because, like Paul, we sometimes do what we hate[28] in a world tainted by sin. Sin can creep up on us in the form of freedom stealers (see the last chapter – unforgiveness, pride etc.)

Getting free from these sins is a process of sanctification and that may take time. God is patient, gracious and merciful, so do the same for yourself and others too (ouch!) After all, most of us have lived with this stuff creating long-term habits for a long time. Whatever time it takes, He will help us to grow, mature and be healed to step (and flow) into the amazing future He has planned.

> *If we [freely] admit that we have sinned and confess our sins, He is faithful and just (true to His own nature and promises) and will forgive our sins [dismiss our lawlessness] and [continuously] cleanse us from all unrighteousness ...*[29]

> *Who forgives [every one of] all your iniquities, Who heals [each one of] all your diseases ...*[30]

If you have had a disagreement with someone, as well as asking God for forgiveness, we also need to ask our friend to forgive us *for our part* in the disagreement, even if they are also in the wrong. Make that call, send that note or meet face-to-face, whatever is necessary to free you up!

> *Confess to one another therefore your faults (your slips, your false steps, your offences, your sins) and pray [also] for one another, that you may be healed and restored [to a spiritual tone of mind and heart] ...*[31]

Once you've taken responsibility and repented, remember that you are in a war zone in a battle for your life and freedom! This fight includes continuing to reject attacks from an enemy who is in business to put you out of business!

reject

As well as sin being a habit that is hard to break in the natural, the Bible tells us that although we live in the natural world, there is a battle going on in the spiritual realm.

> *For we wrestle not against flesh and blood, but against principalities, against powers, against the rulers of the*

> darkness of this world ...[32]
>
> Be well balanced (temperate, sober of mind), be vigilant and cautious at all times; for that enemy of yours, the devil, roams around like a lion roaring in fierce hunger, seeking someone to seize upon and devour.[33]

This other realm may be invisible but it operates at a level just below our conscious surface, and is called theta brainwaves by the scientific community. It's like the thinking before sleep and during meditative states. At this level, thoughts in our mind could be ours, or God's (the Holy Spirit) or darker spirits. It's a battlefield largely waging in our mind. We know from research that negative thinking influences and can cause depression and anxiety disorders[34] whereas positive and uplifting thoughts can potentially change our health.[35]

I believe many of those negative thoughts originate from those dark spirits operating at the theta level of awareness.[36]

The Bible talks about different dark spirits that are not of God. Here is a list of some that I've found. The spirit of fear and timidity (2 Tim. 1:7); of jealousy (Num. 5:14); of perverseness, error and confusion (Isa. 19:14); of prostitution (Hosea 4:12); of impurity (Zec. 13:2); of infirmity (Luke 13:11); of divination (Acts 16:16); of the world (1 Cor. 2:12); of the antichrist (I John 4:3); and of falsehood (1 John 4:6).

Whew! That's a lot of spirits to be aware of, and if you are not used to this theology, the Bible is clear about the enemy of our soul[37] with his fallen angels attacking our freedom in Christ.

Like me you have probably fought some battles. In my teens I was hospitalised for depression. I would often feel this way again in my 20s and 30s. It seemed my situations were hopeless, feeling a burden or a weight over me. As I began to learn more about the spirit world and I let go of sins such as bitterness, anger and unforgiveness, I began to recognise this heaviness often followed negative thinking. I started to speak to the spirit of depression, and the heaviness would immediately leave me as I rejected its influence!

Speak to those negative feelings or worries that are infecting your life and your fruit. *Reject* them as the lies that they are and do it again and again each time your thoughts or actions return to the sin, particularly in challenging times when you struggle and feel weakened.

The next step is where truth becomes freedom. It's simple and achievable when you believe it is possible.

revelation

> ... *with God all things are possible.*[38]

The last step and one of the most freeing and exciting in these Rs to freedom is to ask God in prayer for His truth to receive a divine *revelation*.

This is where all the effort you've done previously; surrendering, fasting, taking responsibility, repenting and rejecting, work together to prepare you to receive God's truth deep in the recesses of your heart. Jesus, by His Holy Spirit, will bring His life-giving revelation to your spirit to replace the lies that you have listened to and believed that took root.

Truth to replace lies. A new healthy root. Yay! A new freedom is on its way.

a prayer of freedom

It is now time to deal with these issues that have kept you bound for too long. If you are ready, be strong, determined and pray the prayer of freedom, which you will find in Appendix 3. You can use it as a model, or reword it for your different situations or use your own heartfelt prayer. The key is to pray in the first person (I repent for …) the R words of *repent, reject* and receive, asking Jesus for His *revelation* for your life and replacing the lies.

After you have prayed, expect to receive His truth and peace. Sometimes we don't immediately sense a revelation as God is often working in the background and in our spirit, so be patient in your wait. He may bring freedom to you through a song heard, a message preached, reading the Word or through other people. However it comes, it will be the direct opposite to the lies you have believed and line up with scripture, bringing a sense of great peace.

Remember Patrick's picture of stepping out of the boat? That was a divine (and biblical) revelation to his spirit.

To help you whilst waiting to receive, I have included scripture truth verses (See Appendix 2) to oppose lies. Your revelation may be contained there!

When you do feel you have heard His divine truth for you, test it against scripture and think about the previously offending emotions. If it no longer causes deep inner pain, most probably God has spoken. Your freedom has begun!!

But look out, there's an adversary that wants you to remain in sin, so continue to reject thoughts and feelings that are old habits and on the way out by replacing with new Word-inspired thinking.

the worst and the best

What happens when you decide to do some spiritual work on the heart and soul? Expect the unexpected.

6 – seize your freedom

All hell breaks loose when godly women make a decision to fight and finally get free so get set for some resistance. Arm yourself with some spiritual support from trusted helpers and get into the Word to stand firm.[39] Being ready for anything is your best attack. Relationships get strained; husbands lose their cool; kids become difficult; health or related weight issues re-surface; finances get stretched with unexpected bills or fines; jobs are lost; self-pity returns. Don't get fearful and crawl back into the safety of the boat (remember it's not really safe in there anyway).

God will bring about change as you remain firm. Remember you are winning this battle. There has been much freedom won. That's the truth.

> ... if the Son sets you free, you are truly free.[40]

Keep fighting. Stand firm. Know and trust your God Who is working on your case. Pray for change. Don't give up. There's movement at the corral. You were always meant to be a woman of beautiful and godly influence as designed by your Creator. So let's get to the beautiful bits shall we? The next section is all about that. Beautiful inside and out, that's you.

before and after

Deanne had a fight on her hands but she didn't initially see it that way. She was convinced her husband was the reason their marriage was in trouble. As a nurse, she was tired of being his nurse now that he was in retirement. Always at his beck and call, whilst struggling to juggle her work commitments, she was becoming physically and emotionally weary of coming home to yet another complaining, sickly person. She was afraid this marriage was failing like her previous two.

All her life Deanne had been searching for love. So far

she hadn't found love or happiness. And she was about to give up on yet another marriage. However it wasn't time to give up. It was time to fight.

Deanne began to take responsibility for her own happiness. As she began a gratitude journal, fasted and dug deep to find unhealthy lies, she repented for the belief that she was worthless. She forgave her husband and asked Jesus to receive a revelation of truth. As a result of her hard work and prayer, God gave her a beautiful revelation of her worth and role to become the encouraging woman God designed her to be.

She worked hard on her marriage and things began to turn around. However things don't always go as we expect and sometimes are not fair. About a year later her husband (quite a bit younger than Deanne) met a younger woman on the Internet and left her.

God had prepared her as she picked herself up after the initial shock. As a strong, godly woman, Deanne is standing in God to look positively towards the future with hope.

Others watching Deanne in the midst of her challenge see a strong, peace-filled, contented woman. That's the flow-on ripple effect of beautiful, godly influence in operation.

short and sweet

- We all search for happiness and love, sometimes in the wrong places, but only God who is Love can satisfy those needs, Rom. 8:39; Eph. 3:19; 1 Thess. 1:4; 1 John 4:16; 1 Cor. 13:4-8.
- Get your bad attitude off your chest by journaling then rule a line to start a new attitude, Ps. 55:22; Jam. 4:6; 1 Pet. 5:7;
- Being grateful and remembering God's help for our lives, reminds us of His love and faithfulness, Ps. 63:1-8, 77:11, 78:35, 111:4.
- Fasting is fantastic for health and spiritual clarity, but firstly get God's leading and don't forget to seek medical advice before you start, Luke 4:2; Acts 10:30.
- Prayer and fasting is about surrendering to and connecting with your Father God and hearing His voice; Ps. 26:2-3; James 4:8,10; Col. 3:1; Luke 2:37, 5:16; Acts 13:1-3; Matt 6:16-19.
- Visit your intense feelings and ask why, why, why, to uncover unhealthy root issues and lies, Deut. 29:18; Matt. 3:10; Mark 4:6; Luke 3:9; John 11:22; Heb. 12:15.
- Lies are those deep beliefs that don't agree with the Bible, Ps. 119:11.
- Jesus helps us to change from sinful ways without condemnation, Rom. 8:1.
- Get help from an experienced counsellor or minister if you need to, 1 Cor. 12:12-29.
- God wants us healed and freed from sin, so we need to take personal responsibility, repent of revealed lies or sins, reject spiritual pull towards sin, to get free, Neh.

9:1-3; Col. 3:5-10; Rev. 3:3; Luke 4:18; John 8:32, 36.

- It's an ongoing fight in an ongoing battle, but in a war that is won, 1 John 2:13.
- Ask God for truth and He will bring revelation in the form of a Bible verse and/or visual picture of a verse accompanied by God's peace. It's His truth if it's backed up by Scripture, 2 Sam. 7:28-29; Gal. 1:12; Eph. 1:17.
- Use the template prayer to take responsibility for the sin of believed lies in your life. Repent, renounce, then ask God for His truth to bring revelation of that truth to counter the lies. Then continue to resist the enemy attacks in the mind in previous sin areas.
- Pray a prayer of freedom and expect change to occur even if it doesn't happen immediately.
- Expect the worst before the best, and stand firm, being a godly influence to others in spite of the battle, 1 Tim. 6:11; John 10:10; Matt. 10:8; Eph. 6:10-18.

journal the journey

- What are you thankful for? Journal your thoughts.
- Talk with God about prayer and fasting. What does He say? What will you do?
- From the feelings chart, what aspects of emotions do you need to visit?
- What are you battles? Check out the following Scriptures for the different types of spiritual beings and battles you might be up against.
- A spirit of fear (2 Tim. 1:7); a spirit of jealousy (Num. 5:14); a spirit of perverseness, error and confusion (Isa.

19:14); a spirit of prostitution (Hosea 4:12); a spirit of impurity (Zec. 13:2); a spirit of infirmity (Luke 13:11); a spirit of divination (Acts 16:16); a spirit of the world (1 Cor. 2:12); a spirit of the antichrist (I John 4:3); and a spirit of falsehood (1 John 4:6).

- What is the worst that could happen as you begin to stand firm in seeing change in your life? What will you do?

a prayer

Father God, it's difficult for me to see my weaknesses and problems that are causing me to sin against you. I submit those areas to you and ask that you would search my heart and point out lies that I believe.

Thank you that in You I have all that I need to fight this battle and win. Lead me towards Your healing as I wait on You.[41]

Un-frazzle & Re-dazzle

peta soorkia

SECTION 3

dazzling influence

Body and soul, I am marvellously made![1]

Strength and dignity are her clothing and her position is strong and secure.[2]

In this section I'm hoping and believing that you will discover your real and perhaps as yet undiscovered beauty. It is much more than your looks or what you wear. It is the heart of a woman – her confidence and a belief in who she is and what she is about. To get to that place, many of us have to do some work to become comfortable in our own skin. Then gradually over time a beauty queen can be unleashed that starts from the inside to work its way to the outside. So let us begin. Get yourself ready to redefine your inner then outer gorgeous self. How exciting!

The previous sections should have helped you find God's peace that surpasses our natural understanding[3] and hopefully removed some of that unwanted baggage you have maybe carried for too long. However, peace and freedom newly discovered are not just for your benefit (really!). God's plan is for them to be shared from what overflows out of you. This is the ripple effect getting more and more powerful, the freer you become.

But wait, there's even more! And it's better still than another set of steak knives. There's more to discover within you. Who me? Yes you, as a beautiful influence.

You may not see yourself as a beauty, but God has an irreplaceable purpose for your influence in this lifetime, that only you can achieve. How you look is a part of that future. This can be achieved by showing on the outside the person who is special and unique on the inside, which is where true beauty begins.

In this chapter, we'll dig inside you a little to discover the most important beauty that every woman has. Inner and true beauty. Then in the next chapter if you choose, how to display that real you on the outside as I cover dressing according to your particular physical shape and skin tone.

7 beautiful inside

What then is beauty? It is defined as "... having qualities that delight which are excellent and wonderful."[4] Are these qualities seen? Or are they things that come from deep within each one of us? Is real and authentic beauty about who we are or how we look?

Come with me as we answer these questions, beginning with how we perceive ourselves.

what we believe

In a fascinating social experiment, an FBI-trained forensic artist spoke with several women and drew two facial impressions of each woman, without seeing them.[5] The first sketch was drawn from their own verbal description of their facial features as he sketched on the other side of a screen. The second was drawn from another person's verbal description. After the sketches were completed, the women were shown their two portraits side by side. Without question, the self-described portraits showed plain uninteresting women. The second ones, drawn as described by other the women they had met for the first time during the experiment, showed vibrant, attractive and beautiful women.

The artist had captured something each woman had. And that was her inner unique personality and vibrancy. The other women had seen it and described it and the artist had drawn it. This 'something' doesn't begin on the outside but is released from the inner person that we are. It's who we really are that is radiated outwardly. Often we don't recognise or value ourselves but many times others do, as illustrated by this account.

What does this tell us? I believe it illustrates that our beauty is indeed in the eye of the beholder and that we see ourselves quite differently. Negatively in fact and definitely not beautiful. Often this is because we feel that we don't measure up in so many ways to that beauty which is portrayed in the media. When we don't believe we measure up, this in turn creates in us an internal lack of self-esteem. This even affects how we see ourselves in the mirror.

I believe that beauty should be about who you are not how you look. And then how you look should be about who you are!

As I write, I have paused to glance at several 4 X 8 lined cards pinned to my bureau desk with encouraging one-liners written by workshop participants. In an exercise we each jot down those visual blips that we don't like about ourselves on one side of a card, then turned over, each card is passed around our table that has five or six other participants for them to note a one-line positive attribute, visual or personal (in bright colours for fun).

One of my cards shows my handwriting and reads: double chin, crooked face, chipped nail, (that was devastating on the day of a big workshop on beauty) and small boobs, (up front and personal). The other sides reads: *lovely smile; happy lady; fantastic sense of style; radiant, colourful,* (yep); *friendly; amazing love and beauty is in you* (I'm tearing up now).

That's what they saw in me. It's different to what I see.

What do you see? How are you beautiful? It's what's in you. Your true gorgeousness, unique woman that you are, is the beauty that is in you. And it is there longing to break out.

In my work with women over many years, I find many women lack personal confidence which impacts on how they see themselves and what they will attempt. As a result it affects who they will become. Whatever their age, if uncertain about themselves, women won't stretch to achieve because they don't believe they possess what it takes to be successful. And for those who know that more is possible, often the willingness to go further is tinged with fear of failure or even fear of success and the responsibility that brings.

All this also affects how they perceive their features. (As shown by my card's comments).

Some women who were told growing up that they would never amount to anything, don't see themselves as attractive. A divorcee single mum I worked with, with special needs children, questioned her natural talent to write, fearing to step out and try writing challenges. She believed she would fail and, due to her divorce that she wasn't beautiful (she is).

After some work, prayer and determination, she began to reinvent her mental picture of herself, recognising the words spoken over her as a child no longer needed to control her thoughts and beliefs. She started to take a few risks, whilst confirming to herself her positive attributes with supportive scriptures. She submitted some stories and articles and some have been accepted so she's feeling better about herself. With some new-found inner confidence, her real personality and eclectic dressing style is being expressed. The real woman, the one on the inside is coming out ... on the outside.

Inner confidence produces inner beauty, which can't help but overflow to the outside.

Here's another story to warm your heart.

Karen was born with a rare condition that caused facial deformities. She has no right ear, thumb or jawbone, was born with a cleft lip and palette, and with a hole in her heart. In the heart-wrenching account on You Tube she tells how she loves her life, work, friends and family and knows that the God who created her loves her just the way that she is.[6] She believes in herself and that it is that beauty that

7 – beautiful inside

overflows from her. She touches lives and inspires women to look for and pursue individual and special qualities, whatever they may be.

Are you perfect? No. Sadly, neither am I. No one but Jesus can claim that. Let us then give ourselves a break. Just like Karen, you and I will never be able to compete successfully with the most gorgeous, intelligent or successful others. We live in a most ordinary world with ordinary tasks to do alongside people – with flaws. Even the most famous women, who seem to have it all together, mess up as they struggle with life's challenges. It's the inner person that depends on God for strength, beauty and love that has a radiating outer glow. That's beauty.

We are all gorgeous as we are and at the same time a work in progress. So like these two women get *your* heart and soul ready to take on a new mindset about who you are. Be prepared to look at life and yourself in a whole new way. Lay aside for a few moments if you can, your past failures, striving for perfection and the trials that have come your way.

Get ready for some attitude changes in order to flourish.

flourishing

What does it mean to flourish? God speaks of it 19 times in the Bible with the Hebrew meaning 'to break forth as a bud, to bloom, blossom, spread, break forth, fly, grow, spring up and extend the wings.'[7]

> *In His days the righteous shall flourish, and abundance of peace, until the moon is no more.*[8]

Flourishing is something beautiful and extremely attractive to others and a whole heap of it is available for us as we stay close to God and His ways.

Brian Houston talks about flourishing in his book, *How to Maximise Your Life*[9]

> "... the countenance of those who are flourishing will be radiant and shine with His joy. Everyone likes to be around such people, and even in the midst of challenges such people maintain their joy ... those who are flourishing will lean towards life ..."[10]

Beautifully described. Even science is researching lives that are flourishing or doing life well, defining it as emotional well-being with positive responses to events and people. People, who love life are generous, forgive, are grateful,[11] and create inner and outer contentment *and* beauty. It is now understood that flourishing can also promote resilience to depression.[12]

I want to flourish. Do you? Wouldn't it be wonderful if others see something special in you and want what you're on!

For me, if I am flourishing now, it's because of what God has done in me over many years and experiences. It wasn't always that way.

inside on the outside

In my early 30s, in the space of just two years, I met Jesus, met and married my husband, and had our first child. For me, from living a *colourful* out-there life, these changes were enormous. As a young mum I remember sitting in the cry-room at our church early in my Christian life, listening to the other mums there who seemed to have it all together. You may recognise them. Mrs Perfect Christian. I, on the other hand, sinner extraordinaire, with nothing going right whilst also feeling like the complete outsider. These mums were mostly stay-at-home mums (fantastic for those who can and want to do that). But I was a mum and felt called to work

7 – beautiful inside

outside the home too!

So there they were. Calm and having it all together. And me! Colourful attire, hair, tights and all. Working mum and not particularly oozing happiness and marriage success and also motherhood challenged. Plus, wearing make-up no less (frowned upon at that time in my denomination but very different now). A square peg in a round hole. Different. On the outer.

What did I do? Who could I come clean with? There didn't seem to be anyone. My husband wasn't aware of my struggles so couldn't help what he did not know about. So I clamped down my personality, shut my mouth and pretended. Did I change my attire? Yes, enough to blend in. Being religious, trying to be and act like the others as a perfect Christian. In the one place where I could have been accepted and loved, I felt alienated from others. If only I had known how to reach out, but my own insecurities prevented that.

It was painful and I didn't know how to move forward. It took years before God could invade my thinking in order for me to stop trying to be someone else. It took internal work (section 2) to understand that to be lovely, I had to be me, real and true to whom God had created and designed from the beginning of time.

Some time after these cry-room days (about 15 years) I had help from my mentor, boss and senior pastor, who was bold (and brave) enough to tell me the truth about many of my blind areas. One of the first things Paul did as he took over our church where I was now part of the pastoral team, was to encourage me to dress and wear my hair to suit my personality. Instead of the sensible Christian version of what I and previous leaders had thought was acceptable as a pastor, I began to relax and allow my inner personality to show. I had been trying so hard to do the right thing. To be a good example. All good. But trying to fit in? Conforming? It was shades of the cry-room.

> ... Don't copy the behaviour and customs of this world, but let God transform you ...[13]

Paul told me the truth about being religious and to let my true inner beauty out. As many tears were shed in his office, the pretence that had built up over many years was slowly but surely discarded. In the process, my hair became more colourful (some say wild, some say cool). And my clothing became more my own style (the rag trade influence sticks). A somewhat eccentric, alternative dresser, or the real me was released. A little bit radical on the inside and a little bit like that on the outside too. A true reflection of me.

These days I'm told I glow. And that is what I desire to share with others who can begin to be themselves too.

In my work now as a coach and in my workshops, I talk with some lovely women of all ages, shapes and sizes. Some might be in emotional or physical pain; others just doing their thing in their day. Those who have inner peace look truly beautiful – particularly when they smile. This and their laughter can lighten any atmosphere. Their smile says to others, *I'm ok even with stuff happening and you can be too.*

Is your inside on your outside? Do you radiate a confidence and beauty without a dependency on your physical looks or lack or expectations of others. Or do you need to remove the pretence? Remember that you don't need to look like the celebrities or the super-models, (usually we can't measure up to those body measurements without major surgery anyhow). And you don't need to be like Pastor so-and-so or the other Christian ladies who *seem* to have it all together. They are working through life's issues just like you and me.

What is it about you that makes *you*? Celebrate that difference. It is after all what makes you truly unique and stunning.

God's dress sense

You are meant to be a radiant, shining, overflowing light in a dim dark world. Not someone in hiding.

> No one after lighting a lamp puts it in a cellar or crypt or under a bushel measure, but on a lampstand, that those who are coming in may see the light.[14]

How then, should that light be displayed? And how does that affect what we should be wearing or not wearing as godly women?

To begin to answer that we'll take a quick look at what, if anything, the Bible says about women and clothes.

> ... And I want women to get in there with the men in humility before God, not **primping** before a mirror or **chasing** the latest fashions but **doing something beautiful for God and becoming beautiful doing it.**[15] (Emphasis mine.)

> Do not let your adornment be **merely** outward – arranging the hair, wearing gold, or putting on fine apparel – rather let it be the hidden person of the heart, with the incorruptible beauty of a gentle and quiet spirit, which is very precious in the sight of God.[16] (Emphasis mine.)

In context, the Apostle Paul in the first verse above, warns the church women not to place their appearance ahead of God. Bible scholars suggest the early-church women written about were trying to impress and flaunt their worth, which tended therefore to exclude others with less wealth.[17]

But the Apostle Peter in the second verse above,

encourages the women to shine not by *only (merely)* the outward looks but mainly through their inner God-given beauty, suggesting that outward decorating is okay as long as this is not the main focus. Anything else such as looks, money, possessions and even family, if placed ahead of our relationship with God, is out of balance.

I believe that you and I are *meant* to shine our inner beauty on the outside like a beacon as a reflection of who He has made us on the inside (our heart) so that *others can see* and *desire* to know where this comes from.

Beauty is also mentioned in the Old Testament. One of the most familiar and remembered story is that of Esther, who we know was beautiful, chosen for that reason. She was encouraged to highlight her beauty to gain the attention of the king.

> *Before each young woman was taken to the king's bed, she was given the prescribed twelve months of beauty treatments – six months with oil of myrrh, followed by six months with special perfumes and ointments. When it was time for her to go to the king's palace, she was given her choice of whatever clothing or jewellery she wanted to take from the harem.*[18]

I wouldn't mind all that pampering! Esther was dressed in finery befitting a queen, with her true beauty not only about the exterior, but also from her inner attractiveness and heart towards God. This attractiveness also flowed from her inner qualities of humility as she dealt with the eunuch and her faithfulness to her uncle Mordecai. I believe that it was these inner attributes that attracted the king once her outer beauty got the king's attention.

Like Esther, people see our outward person first as described in 1 Samuel 16:7 (NLT):

7 – beautiful inside

... People judge by outward appearance ...

In that case then, let us show others what God has put inside us (our personality, strengths and beauty) on our outside.

Esther used her beauty in a good way and dressed beautifully, enhancing her striking features. Let's do the same. If it's good enough for Esther then it's certainly good enough for me!

People are watching. So be free to show the real you beautifully on the outside. If you are an extrovert, dress a little out-there. If you are a gentle, quiet person, then dress in a gentle, soft-coloured way. If you are quiet, dress in confidence with perhaps pastel colours. If you love to have fun, dress in a colourful, fun way. Whatever your personality is, dress appropriately to suit who you *are*. Wear your personality, no longer being ashamed of who you are or how you look.

Enhance your best features, and play down the ones you're not excited about. Perhaps wear some make-up to show those cheek bones, or lipstick to brighten your curved lips. The key is not to rely on it for your inner beauty. Put on your outer beauty to show who you are, then forget it. Don't be preening yourself every minute. Just enhance your natural attributes. People will want what you have – that which is coming from the very heart of you, God's love and peace.

It was once said of me that that I bring colour into a room! And it's true, I love using colour when I dress to enhance my features and show my personality, but I think this statement was attempting to describe me inside and out. (And I'm sticking to this theory by the way). What a beautiful compliment! Where I once used to dress to impress, now I dress to enjoy life, whilst sharing the *me*, whom

God is perfecting. Sharing all the hope and freedom I've been given. That's the colour I want to carry and display each day. You can too!

Can you bring to mind some women you've recently met or known that glow from an inner place? What was so appealing about them? Their smile, or attitude, the way they wore their clothes, the way they related with you? These inner attributes are the things that real inner loveliness is made of. Perhaps their loveliness came from the fact they were themselves. They were real.

I think God is pretty happy with His work. He made us as women and that means beautiful. In fact, you're absolutely drop-dead gorgeous! In fact He says these things about you:

> ... *For we are God's [own] handiwork (His workmanship)* ...[19]

Pretty special hey? If we agree with God, believing that we are specially created and prepared for a purpose, this in my mind is preferable to thinking otherwise. Beauty is intrinsically contained in how we *believe* about who we are and what we're here *for*. We are truly loved by our Creator God and He has put us here on the planet to love Him and show His love towards others. Being beautiful, talented and special is who we are if we would just know it. And it's contained in the deepest part of us, where *true* beauty originates. It's a knowing that we are special with much to offer others. It's not about whether we have or don't have Miss World looks, but about an acceptance of our given features as totally acceptable, God-given and special. This inner *knowing* beauty is *given* by God.

Don't agree with those negative comments from teachers, parents or kids on the school ground. Or perhaps those comments came from other teens, or even from your spouse. Believe the Bible. Believe God. Woman,

7 – beautiful inside

you are beautiful! Remember God who says you are His workmanship and a masterpiece. From this mindset position, you can begin to exhibit and display your individuality. Yours and my looks may not get us on the front page of a magazine but let's do our best to show off God's creation.

Look in the mirror. Smile. Look deeply at you and your smile. Who do you see? See as God sees. Someone that has a unique depth – an inner beauty from a fun, cheeky, exciting, caring or loving personality? Look again. See those inner qualities that no one else has. They are there just below the surface. Remind yourself about those qualities – God-given and prepared for you.

Do you feel a bit better? Commit to believing in your *uniqueness* and beauty today. Remind yourself often that you are indeed *beautiful* in a *special*, God way. And that you are God's *workmanship* (you), that you are *excellent*, that you are *marvellous*, that His thoughts about you are *precious* and that you are indeed *stunning*. I have no doubt that you will achieve great things with these sorts of self thoughts that line up with God's heart.

Read the italicised words from the preceding paragraph once or twice more. Say them out loud preceded by, "I am ..." then insert some God-speak into your heart.

Being truly beautiful is about loving oneself, radiating that to others. The Proverbial woman did.

> *She is strong and graceful, as well as cheerful about the future. Her words are sensible, and her advice is thoughtful. She takes good care of her family and is never lazy. Her children praise her, and with great pride her husband says, "There are many good women, but you are the best!" Charm can be deceiving, and beauty fades away, but a woman who honours the LORD deserves to be praised ...*[20]

I can aspire, as woman, wife, mother and businessperson, to the Proverbial woman's inner charm and grace. That gracious spirit is not man-made but comes from a deep inner knowledge of God.

Don't allow your perhaps difficult life journey or pain or problems or relational issues to define you, as I did. Instead gain strength from any challenges you are experiencing, knowing that you will overcome with God's help. And at the same time, be yourself, develop your personality from the inside onto your outside and enjoy your life so that you can in turn flourish, and be a source of beautiful realness for others to see. He has given you exactly what you need to be the impacting influence you are meant to be. But you must believe in yourself first.

Whatever has been said to you it's time to see, believe and appreciate the best about you. God created you, and He doesn't make mistakes. He is the Master artist and He has created you as a major work of art.

Perhaps you have some physical limitations or other financial or relational circumstances that seem to prevent you from achieving your best. Even with seemingly insurmountable problems or disabilities it is possible to achieve great things with the belief or faith that all things are possible.[21]

And then show it.

getting the beauty out

But *what will I wear?* I can hear your heart cry.

I know. Some of you beauties don't know how to put the pieces together. When it comes to your dressing you find it hard if not impossible and haven't a clue how to begin. Many women shudder when a wedding invitation arrives

7 – beautiful inside

or an interview looms. How should you dress with those body lumps and bumps? And what top would be best with what bottom? (Some of us wish the bottom was a bit more balanced with our top!)

But we can still look good, even with those extra body bits that may have developed when you weren't looking. Don't despair … in the next chapter I will give you practical help in the how-to's of dress sense. What will suit your body shape and show you off to the best? What colours can be worn together and can you wear them? I'll leave the literal dressing to you, but the tips to do it will be my pleasure to share with you to enable you to look great. Even if you do have some or even a lot of natural dress and colour abilities, I hope that there will be something more for you to pick up.

How will you celebrate your qualities and uniqueness in order to flourish, flow, encourage, stand up, extend, love, smile and laugh? Spread your wings. When you are ready it will be time to do those things because the world is waiting for what only you can offer! Let God fill you as a vessel to spill over into the pool that that is your world, creating ever-extensions of lovely inspiration.

Let's now get into the next chapter where you will learn the basics of dressing to help the outside reflect the inner beauty that is *you*.

before and after

Tania didn't believe in beauty, at least not for her. Now middle-aged she had struggled with obesity most of her adult life and as a result, related health issues. Lacking self-esteem when I met her, she also had no clear purpose or direction. She had always believed she was flawed and without value. And definitely not beautiful. This was partially supported by her family and even her church as she remained largely in the background and invisible.

But as an avid Bible reader, I encouraged her to re-examine herself in light of God's words. Her Bible told her that she was valuable and beautiful:

The king is enthralled by your beauty ...[22]

She started to look within herself, to discover who she really was – the real Tania with her own individual uniqueness, beauty and attributes.

On her personal journey she stopped hiding and joined a small group. One of her strengths was that she knew and loved scripture, so with a little bit of assurance that continues to grow, she began to contribute to the discussions. Invisible Tania became visible and with the group's encouragement she began sharing her heart. She started to feel better about herself, more content within, radiating a more appealing persona. Her confidence grew so she decided to try some changes to her appearance.

So she looked in the mirror to discover what was appealing. She noticed that her hair and eyes were attractive so started wearing a little makeup and invested in a good hair style to suit her face shape. As her self-belief and motivation further improved she talked to a dietician about her weight issues. As a result of some weight loss, her health improved.

As Tania started seeing herself in a new light, people began to notice a change in her. They began to include her so she started to serve and volunteer at church.

Tania is still a large dress size but she is becoming more beautiful every day. She just happens to be big and beautiful. Not just big!

She is now in her own small but significant way, impacting her world positively because of who she is. A beautiful influence.

    God says she is lovely and she is beginning to believe it could really be the truth.

short and sweet

- Real beauty comes from within.
- Get a new mindset, agree with God, believe in yourself to influence beautifully, Rom. 12:2.
- Flourish and celebrate your uniqueness, Ps. 72:7; 92:12-13; Prov. 11:28.
- Don't blend in to fit in, be you, Jer. 3:10.
- Be the real you, confident in who you were designed to be, allowing your beauty to be a light shining and overflowing for others to see, Luke 11:33.
- Focus on God in faith, He doesn't make mistakes. This will build your self-confidence, rather than focussing on your limitations and circumstances, Gen. 1:26-31; Heb. 11:1.
- Speak to yourself in faith about your worth, Rom. 10:17.
- Shine for the world to see, Luke 11:33.
- It's okay to dress well on the outside to share the inner person that contains God's hope, peace, joy, freedom and love, Gal. 5:22-23; 1 Pet. 3:3-4.
- True inner and outer beauty comes from God's love for us which is living within us, Eph. 3:14-21.

7 – beautiful inside

journal the journey

- From the verses below, select those that resonate with who you are. Speak them out loud in the first person, i.e., " I am ... God's workmanship." See Ps. 30:11; 45:11, 139:14; 149:5; Prov. 4:9; Isa. 61:3; Eph. 2:10 and 3:20.

- Look in the mirror. Examine your hair, eyes, chin, cheek and other features. What are some of your qualities? How might you enhance those features to show off your godly beauty?

a prayer

Lord, You created me as a masterpiece. A real beauty. Special and for a purpose. Thank you for making me so wonderfully complex and unique.

I desire to shine for You. Help me to develop the beauty you've given me to reflect and show others You.

Thank you Father God, Amen.

Un-frazzle & Re-dazzle

8 beautiful outside

help for the fashion helpless

In the last chapter we looked at finding out who you are on the inside because dressing should be about reflecting that individual person that God has designed. Each one of us is an individual beauty in our own right, whatever our shape, colour or size. As you continue to discover and realise your inner beautiful self, like so many other girls that have been on this similar journey, you may wish to wear outfits that complement that unique God-created woman. I want to point out again in case you missed it, that our beauty begins on the inside. It is God-given and can work its way onto our outside. Let it reflect the beauty within for the world to see.

There is a problem however with this theory. Some girls just don't know how to put the fashion pieces together as it seems too complicated. This was made evident to me recently when I chatted to an attractive young girl (volunteering at a women's conference) and I commented on her pretty dress. She confided that she doesn't have a clue what to wear and that she lacked confidence to try different ways of dressing. This dress was a first and recommended by a friend. Generally she preferred jeans and T-shirts to escape the confusion. I've heard this story from so many girls, young, old, introverted or extroverted, so if you are clothing-clueless, you'll love this chapter.

We will look at body shapes, colour coding, and wardrobe sorting as well as dressing communication.

looking your best

I began my career in the 'rag trade' as it was known in Melbourne in the 70s. Flinders Lane was known as the main fashion centre at that time where designers created for the local market. I began working there after studying fashion then later worked in design, manufacturing, retail, styling and teaching.

With my wide trade experiences, I can say with some degree of confidence that there is no perfect body shape. Fat, thin, tall, short, we are all a masterpiece with individual imperfections.

But in each fashion era there is a perfect 'norm' or a supposedly most pleasing body shape. If you care to study fashion history there were many different body shapes regarded as the 'best' at any particular time. In recent history, the 1800s presented a large, voluptuous, curvaceous silhouette considered beautiful at that time. A slimmer look began to unfold around the turn of the next century with the 1920s lean, long flapper look. In the Twiggy era of the 1970s the fashion profile continued the thin look which is still with us today.

As fashion styles come and go, it is useful for us as Christians to be informed about our community if we desire to live and influence that society. Fashion styling is a part of our world so that if we lived in an Indian, African or Pacific Island nation, we would dress appropriately for that climate and culture, just as we should in the West too.

Fashion styling in our Western world categorises female body shapes as a perfect shape or less than ideal. (Now don't stone me, hear me out). As Christians we are in the world (dressing in the culture we are in), but we are not meant to be of it,[1] which could mean dressing in ways that are without modesty (with low necklines and revealed navels and thighs). We are, I believe, to be in our communities as influencers rather than being influenced and I would like to think perhaps even leading the way … part of the culture where we are not cloned, but instead look and live in a way that is uniquely different.

The Apostle Paul writes:

> I have [in short] become all things to all men, that I might by all means (at all costs and in any and every way) save some [by winning them to faith in Jesus Christ]. And I do this for the sake of the good news (the Gospel), in order that I may become a participator in it and share in its blessings [along with you].[2]

So for me and perhaps you too, we are in a world where we have to dress (cold if we don't), and be a beautiful influence while we're at it. Probably like you, I don't wish to be *of* the world or *ruled* by it where my clothing is my focus. Instead I aim to have fun dressing whilst also showing God's creative genius in creating us as we are, on the outside. And like the Apostle Paul said, becoming all things to all (wo)men!!

In this chapter, there are some styling tips for you to start getting your act (and wardrobe) together in some sort of order. Then, armed with this final piece of the external puzzle with your new peace, freedom and inner beauty, you lady will be dangerous (in the best possible way)! A real God-powered force, shining and overflowing to touch lives.

Here are the practicalities that you've been waiting for. Dressing to look your best.

undressed

To discover the body shape which best describes yours; it's a good idea to get in front of a full-length mirror, wearing some close-fitting clothes, gym wear or underwear. Look objectively at the silhouette or outline of your figure, imagining it as a two-dimensional shape. In your mind's eye, visualise two horizontal lines, one from shoulder to shoulder and the other across the hip from side to side then compare the lengths of these two imaginary lines.

If they are about equal to within 2 cm (¾ inch) and your waist is smaller, then your body shape is said to resemble an hourglass. This is today's 'best' shape as it is evenly proportioned top to bottom with the nipped-in waist. The other shapes are the rectangle, inverted triangle and triangle. These can be camouflaged by clever dressing to resemble the more symmetrical hourglass shape to appear more evenly proportioned. Very few women have the perfectly symmetrical body, but by clever dressing, it can look that way.

Dressing to camouflage any larger or small body parts is about eye movement. A vertical line will often lead a person's eye in the direction of the line. A horizontal shape like a neckline will lead the eye *across* the neck if it is a wide neckline. A coloured sleeve that is contrasted to the body of a top will lead the eye from the sleeve colour to another area of the same colour, perhaps the skirt or the legs.

The brain takes a few seconds to see a whole picture. So when we see anything visual we *look* at and around it as the brain organises and makes sense of what we are seeing. When looking at a clothed person this is no different. We take a moment to view the whole and our eye follows predominantly those lines created by colours and shapes.

Let's now decide on your particular body shape.

shape up

It's of benefit to know which one you fit into so that you can dress accordingly and look your best (to cultural norms). The aim in dressing is to resemble the symmetrical look of the hourglass shape. I will describe each one to see what works and what doesn't work for each.

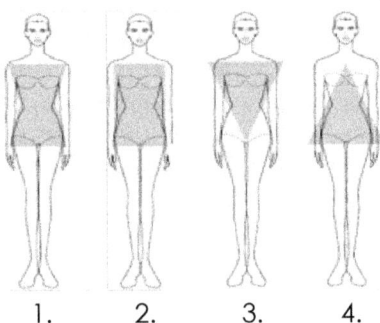

1. 2. 3. 4.

1. the hourglass:

If your two imaginary horizontal lines are about the same visual length comparing the shoulder/breast area with the hip area with a noticeably narrower waist, your shape is said to resemble an hourglass. This is the shape everyone wants and the most desired look whatever your dress size. This one has the most dressing options available.

Hourglass DOs

The hourglass figures can wear any styles so balance your top and bottom halves whilst displaying your best asset – your waist!

Do this by wearing dresses with waistlines, skirts with bands, belt-loops or tabs, or using belts or different coloured tops to bottoms. If you are a smaller frame, wear lighter and multi colours with bright waists; if you are a larger frame, wear darker and single colours with bright waists.

Accentuate your shoulders, bust, waist and hips.

Hourglass DON'Ts

Wearing baggy clothes or short skirts that could make you appear bigger and more rounded than you would like.

2. the rectangle:

If your two imaginary lines across the shoulder/breast area and hips are similar in width and also to your waist, then this is said to resemble that of a rectangle, sometimes described as a brick. (I think I prefer rectangle).

Rectangle DOs

To create the illusion of a curvier shape or the hourglass, an impression of a smaller waistline can be created by using different clothing design lines, features and colours. For the more petite figures, add volume to your hips and bust to create the illusion of curves. Wear fuller tops and bottoms with belts to pull in the waistline. Bring attention by highlighting the shoulder/breast and hip areas with colours, prints, pockets and other details. This will create the illusion of extra roundness whilst making the waist look narrower creating the desired hourglass illusion. For a fuller figure, wear lowered or higher-waisted dresses or tops.

Accentuate your waist (lowered or raised above your actual waistline).

Rectangle DON'Ts

You may wish to avoid vertical stripes or very fitted clothing.

3. the inverted triangle:

If you are wider 2-dimensionally across the shoulder

and breast area than your hip area you are said to be an inverted triangle or apple shape, so the key is to make your top look smaller and your bottom look bigger.

Inverted Triangle DOs

I suggest that you add width to your lower half or the smaller portion of your body, to balance your shoulders, creating the illusion of symmetrical curves. Highlight the bottom half of your body by wearing bright colours, stripes in any direction, lots of details such as pockets, tabs, flaps and baggy pants. If you prefer skirts, wear full or flared styles. These all accentuate, making your shape appear more equal in proportion. Don't wear full tops or coloured or fancy prints, you'll only look bigger. Keep the top of your body in dark or one colour with limited or no details, print, pockets or other trims.

Accentuate your face, hips and legs.

Inverted Triangle DON'Ts

Limit short or cap sleeves or any other details like tabs on sleeves. Don't wear widening necklines, horizontal stripes or shoulder pads on the top half. In fact it's probably wise to forget the bright colours or bold patterns anywhere above the waist. If you must have bright or fashion colours then wear just one colour all over rather than fancy print tops.

4. the triangle:

For this shape, when comparing the visual measures of hip and shoulder/bust area, if the top is smaller, this shape is described as the triangle.

Many women from European ancestry seem to be in this category, myself included. We have big bottoms. My mother used to say, all the better for child bearing. Great, carrying around a big bottom all my life for those hours of pushing.

(Although in the end, it was worth it).

Triangle DOs

Increase the illusion of width or volume across your shoulder/bust area and this will appear to create equal width and balance to your hips. Wear as much colour and detail as you like in tops to bring the eye of the observer from your lower body to expand the width of your upper body. Widen by wearing bright stripes, prints, texture or multi-colours with tops that have lots of interest, details, patterns or wide necks. This will also help to bring attention to your face.

Wear dark colours on your bottoms or a single-colour top and bottom rather than two colours separating pants and tops, whilst keeping the lower areas of the body plain to reduce its apparent size.

Accentuate your face, neck, bust, arms and waist.

Triangle DON'Ts

Wearing horizontal lines across the hip is a big no-no as this will make your bottom look wider. Limit details, such as pockets, trims, contrast colours, texture, or all over prints in pants and skirts.

Now that the main shapes have been covered, you probably want to know how to translate what you've just read to *your* body. Here are a few tips to get you started. Then we will head straight into colour which will have an immediate impact on your appearance.

some shape tips

Once you know your individual body shape, show it to its best advantage by highlighting its strengths whilst playing down the rest. Be adventurous as well as modest. Remember you are shining His light in you.

Regardless of what body shape you may think you are, when deciding on outfits that work or don't work, a good rule of thumb is to try on different outfits with a critical eye. Ask yourself, where is my eye travelling – up, down or across? If you eye moves up and down you will appear taller. If on the other hand your eye moves across, you will seem wider. Do I want to look wider or narrower in some parts? Whatever *your* eye is following, other people's will also.

When shopping, take a friend who dresses with great style and ask for her for honest and objective opinion. It's better to receive the truth from a caring honest friend than to have a wardrobe built on the words of salespeople who may or may not have your best interests at heart. I often shop with girls to help them with their choices and even though I've been involved in the industry, when I shop I sometimes need another opinion too.

Once you have a general idea about your body shape, it would be excellent to know what colours to wear. After all, colour is the first thing that is seen, so it conveys its own message. Your best colours will highlight your individual skin colouring and so enhance your natural glow.

a world of colour

Your personal skin tone influences which clothing colours will look best on you. Some colours will influence your eyes, cheeks and skin tone in positive ways, whilst others will make these same features look less than flattering. You may look alive, younger and rested with some colours or pale, listless or even ill when wearing others. As a general rule, wear your best shades close to your face in tops, scarves or jackets.

Some colour coding disciplines suggest that there are four different types of groupings, but I prefer to simplify using just two, *warm* or *cool* colours. This has its advantages as it's easier to determine which group you belong to. To see a sample set of each colour palette you might like to go to http://www.petasoorkia.com.au/palettes.html as you read this.

Within the grouping that is right for you there will be two or three colours that are the very best colours for you to wear. I call them your signature colours and when you are wearing them you will look and feel a million dollars. I am quite happy to look fabulous if it helps me to appear approachable, friendly and different to those searching for answers. I'm sure that like me, instead of aspiring to worldliness in our appearance with our individual style, we can choose to be a Christian beacon.

There are different pigments that create our skin tones, and each person has a different combination of these pigments. Generally different cultural groups have similar pigments, for example, African, Indian, Chinese, or Irish descent can belong to the same colour grouping, even though their colourings are very different.

People with warm skin tones reflecting more tones of yellow and gold, like our former woman Prime Minister, Julia Gillard, often come from Celtic or Scottish heritage. On the other hand, people with cool tones, reflecting tones of blue and pink skin, can be both the darker skinned people-groups and fairer groups. An example of someone with cool undertones is Kate, Duchess of Cambridge (Prince William's wife).

To decide your colour grouping, try to find some plain-coloured scarves or fabrics including black, white, cream and brown. Make sure they are solid one-colour pieces. You might also try to have some other assorted plain colours available too. The more colours you try the easier it will be to recognise your colour group.

Armed with your colours, find yourself a spot facing a mirror, preferably in natural light, wearing little or no make-up with your hair away from your face. Sometimes dyed hair can make it difficult for correct colour recognition.

Drape the scarves or fabric colours one at a time around your face, covering your clothing. With each colour, examine your facial features for brightness of eyes, light or shadow underneath eyes, any natural flush of cheeks and the healthy glow of your face. You should be looking at your eyes and face to see the reaction of your skin to the colours rather than observing or looking at the colours themselves.

If your face looks brighter with the white and black scarves, this means these represent the best colour group for you to wear. In other words, you have *cool* skin tones. Cool baby! If on the other hand the cream and brown make you look better, fresher, younger (cool or warm, we all want that please) then *these* are your colours. And in this case you have *warm* skin tones.

In each colour grouping, there is a wide range of colour options, just a few of which are shown at my web site. But this small palette is by no means exhaustive; in fact there are thousands in each group, some of which will be your particular best colours within either the cool or warm group. Discovering which particular ones are your very best or signature colours is through the same trial process. If you have other plain scarves or articles of clothing, you can examine those in the same way you draped the white and black versus the cream and brown scarves. If you don't have any of these, visit a fabric store and view a range of plain colour fabrics held up to your face. Check out which ones make your face look the very best.

My signature colours are red, purple and pink, which I use as my *accent* colours when dressing. Most girls have two to four best signature colours. Black, navy, grey and white are my *classic* or *neutral* colours for basic items and my wardrobe reflects this. Whenever I'm shopping, I simply scan the shop with my eyes to find my colours. I investigate the store if I spot the right shades, or I walk on if I don't. Makes life and shopping much easier.

The two colour palettes shown are examples of some of the colour shades you may be able to wear; these are not exhaustive or absolute. They will simply give you some idea of colours for your particular colour group. You can imagine adding black shades or white hues to a cool colour or brown or cream for warm tones as in a paint palette, to increase the possibilities. The new, darker and lighter colours produced could all work for your colour group.

cool baby cool

Cool colour DOs

Wear colours near your face that have cool tones. In other words, containing blue undertones. These include white, black and the primary colours plus pastel tints of these brights. Cool tones usually have predominantly clear white-based backgrounds.

Cool colour DON'Ts

Don't wear cream, brown or any of the autumn colours near your face. If you love these colours or if they are in fashion and you must have them in your wardrobe, then by all means wear them but drape a scarf or wear tops of the 'right' colours next to your face.

warm and cuddly

Warm colour DOs

Wear autumn colours near your face, such as cream,

brown, khaki, mustard, pinkish-maroon, yellow-reds, burnt orange.

Warm colour DON'Ts

Try not to wear any cool tones near your face such as white, black or other colours which are blue or white-based. If you do want to wear any cools then I suggest you put them on the lower section of your body, below the waist, using scarves, accessories and tops in warm tones to surround your face.

some colour tips

You may have noticed that some colours feature in both cool and warm palettes, for example red and navy. Many other colours such as purple, yellow, orange, greys, even some browns can have both warm and cool shades. As a general rule, the cool colours are sharper and brighter and the warmer colours usually more muted towards autumn tones.

To determine if a colour suits you when shopping, duplicate the cool or warm test described above. Take the item you like into the change room along with a known colour that suits you from the shop (white or black for cool skin, cream or brown for warm skin). Drape each, one at a time, to critically examine your face. Check the difference. No good? Or do you look beautiful, fresher, 10 years younger? Yes? Quick, try it on, snap it up to confidently add to your wardrobe.

Even with years of design and fashion experience under my belt, when shopping I still do the check-the-right-colour-test, although often I have a fair idea of what will or won't work just by looking at the colour. With practise over time, you will also be able to quickly scan the racks for your colours before heading anywhere near the change rooms. Shop like this and you'll find yourself looking and feeling more confident about how to dress and how you appear.

It's also very helpful to have a second opinion such as a girlfriend with you when shopping. (Maybe your male friends or husbands may not want to tell you the truth for fear of getting into trouble! Or if they are like my husband they would rather be anywhere else than shopping with you.)

In time, applying these practical colour tips, you will probably find that you have two or three 'best' colours that work very well with your skin colouring. From these colours you can begin to build your wardrobe, so that it becomes more colour-coordinated with less clutter of unwanted and unworn clothing.

Knowing what enhances your shape and your best colours, you're almost ready to fly to the shops. But just a moment. Something requires your attention first.

your wardrobe sorted

The one place in a home that can intimidate and put fear into the hearts of women is the wardrobe.

Many girls despair over it and it makes husbands shudder and roll their eyes. It's a place that often gets deposits without many withdrawals. And it seems that there is never anything in it to wear.

So it's time. You and I can sort what might be your disaster area. Clothes shopping will become a breeze once you've emptied your wardrobe of unnecessary items. Believe me, once you have executed this next step, your wardrobe will seem to speak volumes by what's missing.

To prepare, set aside a few of hours with an honest friend for help and some supplies for stamina and courage

(chocolates and caffeine?)

In addition to your friend and the supplies, have some large garbage bags on hand.

If you are a hoarder and can't bear to be parted from those clothes that haven't seen the light of day for years you'll find this next task difficult. That's why your friend should be chosen with care. Truth is her best asset and your good fortune.

To begin. Answer this question for each piece of clothing; *have I worn this outfit within the last 12 months?* Whatever the answer, each item will go into one of three heaps or groups with one group rehung and the others eventually into a bag. Ask it each time, and believe me, you will benefit if your friend is lovingly firm and kind when she helps you cull your unworn clothing.

When sorting this way, if the answer to this all important question is no, because it needs some minor or major alterations then add it to the revamp group.

Requiring revamping:

This group can significantly improve your wardrobe with just a little bit of effort, adding items you might not have worn for some time.

Perhaps a top needs a new button or a skirt needs the hem raised, or lowered. A dress or jacket needs the side seams taken in or out. Whatever the need, do something with each item straight away to get them back into your wardrobe quickly. If you sew, place these on that machine until you get to them or take them to a clothing alterations pop-up shop in shopping centres. Get this bundle into your car for the next time you're out and about. You could get tired of moving them around the car so they may end up in a recycle bin somewhere –as long as they don't go back in the wardrobe.

The second group items have probably seen better days ... a very long time ago! They are destined for the discard heap to exit your wardrobe and life forever!

Someone else's new pre-loved clothing:

You might love it and it might have sentimental memories attached but it's time to let it go (you are allowed to keep your wedding dress, or one or two other sentimental items). For those pieces that are too small, it's time to recognise that you may never be a size 6 again. Unfortunately neither will I. Out it goes! (Quickly before you change your mind).

Another reason you may have been holding onto a beautiful item is that it looked so perfect in the shop window and the sales assistant told you it was 'made for you' but you have never been comfortable to put it on. Why? It's probably the wrong colour, or shape for you, as simple as that. Now you have the knowledge, get over it, let it go and chuck it out. In the process maybe you are helping (influencing?) a woman you may never know, with a beautiful new addition to *her* wardrobe.

And now your wardrobe breathes a sigh of relief.

The third group, you have worn and you love and you look great in them.

Yours to keep:

They go back. Hallelujah. Something you can actually wear!

Chances are your wardrobe is now looking a little leaner and uncluttered, particularly if your (ruthless) friend lived up to her reputation. Time for a well-earned break (is there any chocolate left?)

Have a critical look now at what you've got. Group your

similar items together, all your bottoms together, skirts and pants, etc., then the tops, long-sleeved, short-sleeved shirts and jackets together. Put dresses and jumpers and others in item groups and if you want to you could colour group as well.

Suddenly there will be obvious gaps in your wardrobe. This is wardrobe talk. It sounds like this. *I am missing things.*

Perhaps there's no little black dress or basic jacket. Perhaps you have lots of floral tops and no plain-coloured ones. Maybe you don't have any long-sleeved blouses or knitwear, and hopefully this is now quite evident.

Make a list of what you need then think about the colours. Perhaps they need to be in your signature colours or accent brights or maybe the neutrals. In Appendix 4, you can plan for your shopping trips. Now you can plan your wardrobe.

Next, after the hard work comes the exciting part. More wardrobe talk. *Someone needs to go shopping.* Someone has to do it! And it may as well be *you*.

Begin to invest in some good quality items for trans-seasonal wear. These are clothes that can be worn in a variety of different seasons or weathers. Have this list with you when the sale items start calling your name from the clothes racks. If it's the wrong colour, shape, price or item for *your* wardrobe – walk away!

Think about your wardrobe as investing in the expression of you. A beautiful, glowing and ever-rippling *you*. Think about having two types of investment groups as you build your wardrobe. The first contains your basics. Decide how much you can afford to spend/invest on these longer-lasting trans-seasonal quality items in your classic or neutral colours such as black, navy, brown, grey, white or cream. You might need to save up for these so choose carefully. For the second group, spend less money but more often, perhaps in each season. These are the current-trend items, such as bright, printed or colourful pieces to bring highlights and interest to the more classic and more expensive items from the first group.

You don't need to spend a lot of money on your wardrobe but you do need to spend wisely. If you are like me and love the second-hand shops and clothes swap parties, you can look great inexpensively. As you slowly build up your wardrobe, you are investing in you, your look and as a by-product, your influence. Buying slowly and deliberately means that all the pieces should match, should fit, and over time will support each other. The type of clothing that should be included in your wardrobe will depend on you and your particular lifestyle.

How do you now translate all of that information onto your precious little exterior self and exit your front door, looking and feeling like a million dollars?

Here is a guide to the fun process of dressing up.

some dressing tips

- Be you. Be real. Dressing and clothes should be fun and be about proclaiming with fun, and dignity, who you are and whose you are.

- Work out what you're going to wear before you get dressed, preferably at another time. I get my clothes ready the night before. For a special occasion, a week or more prevents last-minute mayhem and disasters, not to mention expense as you rush out and buy in a panic.

- Investing in tops and bottoms gives more value for your dollar. Three tops plus three bottoms can potentially produce nine outfits. Three, four, five or six dressess, equal exactly the same number of outfits.

- Each time that you prepare an outfit, select one piece such as a pant, jacket, or pair of shoes that you want to wear and build the outfit from that.
- You could try on the outfits as you plan if you have the time. Take photo shots of outfits that work for future reference.
- Balance colour and shape using the natural movement of the eyes which tend to follow similar colours and line movements.
- As you try pieces together, check exactly how your eye is moving. As a result of those eye movements, do you appear slimmer or wider?
- For your body shape, aim to extend and widen your narrowest part whilst at the same time narrowing the widest areas using colours and lines to produce a balanced top and bottom (hour-glass).
- The eye usually follows lines. Lines can be stripes or seams or lines produced where skin meets fabric.
- Or is the eye following the colours? The eye will join colours together. For example a black top will make the eye move down to the feet to follow black shoes.
- Try different combinations of clothing to see what the eye does.

Remember that your dressing is often the first thing people see, then your actions and last but not least, your words. And they are all about communicating who you are to the ocean that is your world.

8 – beautiful outside

dressing speaks

Is it important to you that others want to listen to what you have to say? (My answer is yes please, particularly my husband – he listens if I remember to divide my word count by 10!)

Seriously, did you know that research suggests that clothing has a *major* impact on what people think about us.[3] This verse keeps popping up in this book; here it is again just to remind you.

> ... *For the Lord sees not as man sees; for man looks on the outward appearance, but the Lord looks on the heart.*[4]

And who that person is inside, and what we believe about ourselves, has a significant impact on how we communicate and the way we project to those around us. This includes our body language, or how we speak, smile, stand and even look at people.

In other words, people make the most lasting impression from the visual image that we present, followed closely by our body language. Surprisingly our words feature last when making a first impression. It seems odd doesn't it? Particularly when our words are so important.

> *Let your conversation be gracious and attractive so that you will have the right response for everyone.*[5]

Words are important to me and probably to you too. I really want the words that I speak to be taken seriously by those I work, live or do life with. If this is also important to you, and you want to be heard by people at interviews, work, home, community, church, school or uni, then dressing appropriately whilst projecting a godly confident personality, will assist people to *listen* and *hear* *what* you say with your words.

What do you want to communicate? Are you getting ready for a big selling pitch, or a presentation at school or work? Or are you preparing to talk with other parents at school, to a group or an important talk with one special person? In preparing, how you look, what you wear and how you speak is as just as important as what you say.

As God helps you fix up your inside with peace and freedom, and you dress up your outside, you can allow your words to do the rest.

> *No one lights a lamp and then hides it or puts it under a basket. Instead, a lamp is placed on a stand, where its light can be seen by all ...*[6]

Wearing well-shaped and coloured clothing could influence those people at your next job interview, your next preaching message or even your next date (definitely that one).

In conclusion, you have now studied your body at length in the mirror, checking out your body shape and colours, and you have some ideas about how to make the big bits a bit smaller and the little bits a bit bigger.

Any woman (you and me included) can make the most of the body God has given her. Large, small, tall, short, we are all a masterpiece regardless of imperfections.

And right now I pray that you have moved a little closer towards knowing who you are inside and that the real you is emerging. I pray that you would be excited to display that flourishing woman, distinctively created and styled by your Maker – all in the name of beauty and shining the light to overflow to a world that needs you!

before and after

Elle's body was still a perfect hour-glass shape but with

the birth of her third child she had increased from a size 14 to 20. An extrovert in personality, she and her husband were struggling with finances, work, family and church pressures. So the always-out-there fun person she had been was now challenged in many areas, including her body image.

She saw only fat, flab and drab when she looked in the mirror and this was reflecting outwards to her world. As money was tight, she didn't know how to begin to revamp her wardrobe.

Elle needed some dressing help and encouragement to feel better about herself in order to display her natural outgoing personality, given her current appearance and circumstances.

She re-examined what God says about her in the Bible, and remembered how special she is to Him (size 12 or 20) and made a decision to reflect her godly uniqueness in her personal look even with her current size. She began to accept who she is, rather than who she wants to be. A great choice.

Elle then did some practical things to further enhance her inner and outer self-confidence by working out her signature colours (cool) with an hourglass shape. She sorted her wardrobe, throwing out those size 12 clothes and invested in some inexpensive fun pieces as she could afford them. In what had been for some years a drab wardrobe, new life was injected, producing something that resembled her engaging individuality.

To date, with a small amount of funds, she has invested in some crazy and beautiful black and white striped leggings as contrasts, a black skirt, a red top and a black styled and beautifully cut jacket to suit her outgoing qualities.

She looks fabulous and you definitely wouldn't miss her in a crowd. She looks very much the delightful young woman that she is, unreserved and beautifully attractive from inside reflected on her outside. She is saying to the world, *here I am as I am – round, cuddly and special.*

This is beauty. It shines, overflows, for the whole world to see. And it's contagious.

short and sweet

- Some women don't know how to dress well. There is information here to help.
- Shine your light to overflow what is within, Ps. 112:4.
- How you appear to others is about being seen in their eyes. Show off who God created inside and outside, 1 Sam. 16:7.
- God has created you as a unique individual beauty in this time and place, so dress according to your individual personality and environment, Est. 2:13.
- Be a part of the local culture when dressing in order to be an influence to others, but be *the you that God made* rather than copying others, Eph. 1:4, 18, 2:10, 4:7, 16, 5:1, 15.
- Work out your body shape by examining your silhouette in a mirror comparing your shoulder, waist and hip width.
- The hourglass figure is a symmetrical body shape, with other shapes using visual camouflaging to resemble the hourglass.
- Get a friend's advice to help you shop for clothes that work for your figure type, Eccl. 4:12; Prov. 17:17, 27:6.
- Wearing the best colours near your face that best suit your skin tone will help you look and feel better.
- Discover your colours by draping scarves or fabric near your face to see which complement your colouring.
- Weed out your wardrobe with the help of your trusted friend and the 12-month wearing test, separating your clothes into: *requiring revamping; someone else's new pre-loved clothes;* and *yours to keep.*

- To build your wardrobe, spend and choose wisely, treating each purchase as an investment in your personality and a way to shine His light, Prov. 2:2-11.
- When shopping, look for those colours that you wear in your wardrobe before you try anything on and then compare in the cubicle mirror with one of your signature colours.
- In today's world, communicating a message begins with our image, how we project followed by what we say. Let it all be godly, Rom. 15:5-6.
- You can become more approachable to those who are seeking answers in their lives as they see you as a bright, cheery and alive light for Jesus, Matt. 28:19.
- Prepare beforehand what you will wear, checking for balance, your particular style and eye movement.

journey journalling

- What body shape are you? What areas would you like to enhance and which ones would you like to tone down a little?
- Are you a cool baby or warm and cuddly?
- Do you know your signature colours? Perhaps schedule a date with a trusted and honest friend to help you decide on your shape and skin tones and best colours.
- Schedule another date to cull your wardrobe. Make it a fun event with a couple of girlfriends who may be a similar size. They may love your cast-offs and give you a helping hand into the bargain.
- After looking at the wardrobe planner in Appendix 3, what are your wardrobe goals? Set a time and

financial goal to change the state of your wardrobe and as a result how you look.

- Do you have an important meeting or a particular message to convey? How do you think you should dress to support your message?

a prayer

Thank you Lord that you made me in Your image and perfect in your sight. May I be who You made me to be without trying to be someone I'm not. I desire to be a light for You and reach others as a living example of Your beauty, love and grace. Amen.

Un-frazzle & Re-dazzle

9 — the best influence

> ... *Let no one ever come to you without leaving better and happier. Mother Teresa of Calcutta.*[1]

let it flow

I trust that by now you have un-frazzled much of your frazzle in God's sweet presence; that you are learning who you are so that the real you is emerging and you are beginning to display that dazzling woman created and styled uniquely by your Maker.

Some years ago, I met a charming woman at a weekend retreat who displayed strength and godly influence and we arranged to meet. Justine's husband drove her down to Melbourne from their country home on a hot blustery summer's day so that the two of us could spend a few hours getting to know each other. It was a generous act as they pastor a vibrant and busy church and probably had much to do.

I found her story compelling. She told how strife had hit her home when depression fell on her husband after key people, his best friends, had left their church some years before, causing division and discord on their way out. The role of Senior Pastor is demanding and I've heard many stories of pastors who are no longer in active ministry positions in Australia. On the day that he got the news, her pastor husband (in shock as a type of paralysis hit him), rang her at the school where she works as a teacher. In ministry, or in fact in many helping roles, it's not uncommon to suffer burnout from overwork and never-ending people challenges.

Justine's husband's brain switched off due to the high levels of stress, so that he had no idea how to proceed forward. He was totally physically and emotionally traumatised and immobilised by the bitter way the

9 – the best influence

separation had occurred.

This woman of influence took the reigns as she sought out her own peace and serenity from her Source, God, so that her husband wouldn't fall into full depression. She gave him suggestions and strategies every day as she left her place of work and met him for lunch. At the same time, she dealt with her own hurt and pain that she carried in order to forgive, release and love the offenders. After all, she reasoned after time in prayer, we are all a work in progress, often hurting others through our own inner pain and unmet needs.

She did the three things that this book has covered. She connected with her peace-giving God, she did internal adjustments to release her own burdens and she found her beauty and strength within as she allowed that to flow through her.

Her husband had never seen a more beautiful sight those lunch times – his steady, strong, encouraging and loving wife who still believed in him, even when he didn't. She reassured him of his worth and value.

Like Justine's life, our lives can positively impact those close to us or those that we interact with as we go about our daily lives. Instead of being negatively affected by other people's difficulties and negative outcomes, no matter how close they are to us, like Justine we can dig deep to change ourselves within by the power of the Holy Spirit. God changed her and she positively impacted her husband and, as a result, this couple continue to touch lives in their church and the wider community.

In the midst of a mad world you and I can find our peace in Him. We can take off the mask of pretence, to become genuine and unload our baggage. We can recognise our own beauty – the beauty that is inside that connects to the uniqueness of you, and who God sees. We can exhibit that exquisiteness on the outside by beginning from the inside. Glowing and overflowing. Re-dazzled in fact!

There are women like Justine if you look around. Like those from the recent or distant past who operated from their godly strengths within to change a world. Women such as Victoria Osteen, Darlene Zschech, Beth Moore, Elisabeth Elliot, Mother Theresa, Marilyn Hickey, Aimee Semple McPherson, Corrie ten Boom, Catherine Booth and Florence Nightingale. You might even look within yourself to find one too.

The Maker of the universe is standing by to pour something supernatural into us as we remain open to receive in that peaceful place. As women who dare to take up the challenge to continue to develop and grow, leaning on our Saviour, we can literally change everything.

We can be the vessels filled with His love overflowing into a pool called life. As His poured essence flows into us, ripples extend from us to our world and beyond further than we can comprehend. Look in the mirror at yourself. You, my inspiration, are a woman of influence.

> ... a woman who honours the LORD deserves to be praised ...[2]

a love waltz

The Choreographer has the moves perfected and as the Dancer-Leader, He leads you on the dance floor of life with grace and care. He has orchestrated the dance so that you learn on the floor as you're guided gently in the moves. His touch is firm, yet ever leading you onwards, forwards, upwards in the dance.

Your heart is moved by the beauty and skill of the Dancer whilst your spirit soars to the music. You notice that the audience is watching as your movements sway with the Dancer in perfect time. If your thoughts are distracted, your steps falter. They see. They watch.

You glow. Something flows from you. Your beauty is unmatched except for His. Your eyes are on Him and His eyes are on you. And they watch. They see the beauty, they receive from the flow and they want to dance too.

Let the Choreographer lead. Let Him direct. His steps are the Way, the Truth and the Life.

a prayer

> *Thank you Lord for Your influence in my life. It enriches me, it empowers me, it lifts me, it strengthens me because you love me. And I love you.*
>
> *As I recognise your Spirit guiding and leading to share what I have and who I am, may I overflow so that You can direct the ripples ever-outward.*
>
> *Amen.*

Un-frazzle & Re-dazzle

appendices

APPENDIX 1

SCRIPTURES FOR GM DE-STRESS

There are many meditative verses in the Bible that you can use to relax and find peace. The Psalms or Proverbs are great sources – choose one of these or search for one that gives you a serene and calm impression. Listed here are some of my favourites.

Then the Lord God formed man from the dust of the ground and breathed into his nostrils the breath or spirit of life, and man became a living being. Gen 2:7 AMP

The Lord is my Shepherd .... He makes me lie down in [fresh, tender] green pastures; He leads me beside the still and restful waters ... Ps 23:1-2 AMP

... I will guide you along the best pathway for your life ... Ps 32:8 NLT

Take delight in the Lord, and he will give you your heart's desires. Ps 37:4 NLT

Let be and be still, and know (recognise and understand) that I am God ... Ps 46:10 AMP

Our lives are in His hands ... Ps. 31:15 NLT

Those who live in the shelter of the Most High will find rest in the shadow of the Almighty. Ps 91:1 NLT

... the Lord, He is my Refuge and my Fortress, my God; on Him I lean and rely, and in Him I [confidently] trust! Ps 91:2 AMP

For He will order His angels to protect you wherever you go. Ps 91:11 NLT

appendices

The Lord keeps watch over you as you come and go ... Ps 121:8 NLT

You chart the path ahead of me and tell me where to stop and rest ... Ps 139:3 NLT

You go before me and follow me. You place your hand of blessing on my head. Ps 139:5 NLT

I will keep thinking about Your marvellous glory and Your mighty miracles. Ps 145:4 CEV

The Lord ... showers compassion on all his creation. Ps 145:9 NLT

He will feed His flock like a shepherd; He will gather the lambs with His arm, And carry them in His bosom, And gently lead those who are with young. Isa 40:11 NKJV

But those who wait for the Lord [who expect, look for, and hope in Him shall change and renew their strength and power... Isa 40:31 AMP

For I the Lord your God hold your right hand; I am the Lord, who says to you, Fear not; I will help you! Isa 41:13 AMP

O Lord, You are our Father; we are the clay, and You our Potter, and we all are the work of Your hand. Isa 64:8 AMP

Give all your worries and cares to God, for he cares about you. 1 Pet 5:7 NLT

Peace I leave with you, My peace I give to you; not as the world gives do I give to you. Let not your heart be troubled, neither let it be afraid. John 14:27 NKJV

APPENDIX 2

SCRIPTURE TRUTH

Depression

Restore to me the joy of Your salvation and uphold me with a willing spirit. Ps. 51:12 AMP

... Don't be dejected and sad, for the joy of the Lord is your strength! Neh. 8:10 NLT

Fear

For God did not give us a spirit of timidity (of cowardice, of craven and cringing and fawning fear), but [He has given us a spirit] of power and of love and of calm and well-balanced mind and discipline and self-control. 2 Tim. 1:7 AMP

Lean on, trust in, and be confident in the Lord with all your heart and mind and do not rely on your own insight or understanding. Prov. 3:5 AMP

Guilt/ Shame

The godly may trip seven times, but they will get up again. Prov. 24:16 NLT

There is therefore now no condemnation for those who are in Christ Jesus, who walk not according to the flesh, but according to the Spirit. Rom. 8:1 KJ21

Hopelessness

But those who wait for the Lord [who expect, look for, and hope in Him] shall change and renew their strength and power; they shall lift their wings and mount up [close to God] as eagles [mount up to the sun]; they shall run and not be weary, they shall walk and not faint or become tired. Isa. 40:31 AMP

Return to the stronghold [of security and prosperity], you prisoners of hope; even today do I declare that I will restore double your former prosperity to you. Zech. 9:12 AMP

No eye has seen, no ear has heard, and no mind has imagined what God has prepared for those who love him. 1 Cor. 2:9 NLT

And all these blessings shall come upon you and overtake you if you heed the voice of the Lord your God. Deut. 28:2 AMP

The thief comes only in order to steal and kill and destroy. I came that they may have and enjoy life, and have it in abundance (to the full, till it overflows). John 10:10 AMP

So all of us who have had that veil removed can see and reflect the glory of the Lord. And the Lord – who is the Spirit – makes us more and more like him as we are changed into his glorious image. 2 Cor. 3:18 NLT

Loneliness

He [God] Himself has said, I will not in any way fail you nor give you up nor leave you without support. [I will] not, [I will] not, [I will] not in any degree leave you helpless nor forsake nor let [you] down (relax My hold on you)! [Assuredly not!] Heb. 13:5 AMP

A father of the fatherless and a judge and protector of the widows is God in His holy habitation. Ps. 68:5 AMP

What then shall we say to [all] this? If God is for us, who [can be] against us? [Who can be our foe, if God is on our side?] Rom. 8:31 AMP

Astray thinking

... we lead every thought and purpose away captive into the obedience of Christ (the Messiah, the Anointed

One).. 2 Cor. 10:5 AMP

Stress and Anxiety

Let be and be still, and know [recognise and understand] that I am God. Ps. 46:10 AMP

Don't worry about anything; instead, pray about everything. Tell God what you need, and thank him for all he has done. Phil. 4:6 NLT

Casting the whole of your care [all your anxieties, all your worries, all your concerns, once and for all] on Him, for He cares for you affectionately and cares about you watchfully. 1 Pet. 5:7 AMP

Worry weighs us down; a cheerful word picks us up. Prov. 12:25 MSG

Peace I leave with you; My [own] peace I now give and bequeath to you. Not as the world gives do I give to you. Do not let your hearts be troubled, neither let them be afraid. [Stop allowing yourselves to be agitated and disturbed; and do not permit yourselves to be fearful and intimidated and cowardly and unsettled.] John 14:27 AMP

You will keep in perfect peace all who trust in you, all whose thoughts are fixed on you! Isa. 26:3 NLT

Unlovable

There is no fear in love [dread does not exist], but full-grown (complete, perfect) love turns fear out of doors and expels every trace of terror! 1 John 4:18 AMP

I will confess and praise You for You are fearful and wonderful and for the awful wonder of my birth! Wonderful are Your works, and that my inner self knows right well. Ps. 139:14 AMP

APPENDIX 3

A PRAYER OF FREEDOM

Here's a prayer that includes the R-words (see chapter six) which you may like to use once you have uncovered any lie-based beliefs or sin operating in your life. You can use it as a model, rewording it for your particular situation.

> Father God, thank You, You made me, You love me unconditionally and Your grace is all I need. Father, I take responsibility for engaging in any ugly wrongdoing or sin in my life knowingly or unknowingly.
>
> I repent of this/these and ask that You forgive me for the sin/s of _____
>
> and/or believing the lies about myself such as
>
> _____
>
> I forgive _____ and release them from my judgement. Father, forgive me for any unforgiveness and the judgements that I have.
>
> I also ask forgiveness for the sin/s of _____ on behalf of my extended family past, and future generations, and that you cleanse unrighteousness from my family tree past, present and future. As a believer of Christ, I stand in the gap for those that don't know Your freedom and love.
>
> I reject these sins _____
> in the name of Jesus Christ.
>
> Holy Spirit, strengthen me to resist the habits of sinful thoughts and actions that are ungodly and help me to be aware of attacks on my freedom.
>
> Jesus, I ask to receive Your revelation of Your truth to replace the lies of _____, in your precious name,
>
> Amen.

APPENDIX 4

WARDROBE PLANNER

In this wardrobe planner, write down the number of items you have in the appropriate column to see where the spaces are. Fill in what you need with your colour choice. Now you are ready to shop.

	DRESSES	BOTTOMS	TOPS	SHOES
CASUAL				
ACTUAL				
NEED				
NEED				
BUSINESS				
ACTUAL				
NEED				
NEED				
SPORTS				
ACTUAL				
NEED				
NEED				
AFTER 5				
ACTUAL				
NEED				
NEED				

APPENDIX 5

MEETING JESUS FACE-TO-FACE

Who is this God who seems to radically change people?

When I first met Jesus I knew immediately that I was unconditionally loved and accepted and that He had an amazing plan for me. Before this experience I had believed that I was okay, but my actions showed that I was searching in the wrong places for answers. Men friends, travel, recreational drugs, career, money and possessions – anything to help me find fun and a life purpose.

Then, one day, I received a huge dose of hope, security, peace and so much more as I came face-to-face with Jesus. Nothing before or since has so rocked my world in such a significant way. I became born again and was changed from the inside out.

Put your faith in Jesus. He's waiting for you.

… Here I stand at the door and knock. If you hear me calling and open the door, I will come in… Rev. 3:20 NLT

If you want that, it's as simple as praying like this:

Jesus, be my Lord and Saviour. I believe you are the Son of God, that You died and rose from the dead. I need You today. Forgive me my mistakes and make me a new person, Amen.

If you prayed that prayer for the first time or after being away from Him, contact me at www.petasoorkia.com.au or get into a welcoming Bible believing church to help you on your new faith journey.

END NOTES

INTRODUCTION

1. Est 4:14
2. Definition of influence paraphrased from the Encarta Dictionary, (U.K.)
3. Gen 3:4-6 NKJV
4. Est 4:14-14 NLT
5. 1 Sam 25:3 NIV
6. 1 Sam 25:33 NIV

CHAPTER 1

1. Phil 4:7 UKNIV
2. John 14:27 NKJV
3. Phil 4:7
4. www.oxforddictionaries.com/definition/english/stress: Retrieved, 11 Jul, 2015.
5. Flaxman, P., E., & Bond, F., W., (2010) Worksite stress management training. Journal of Occupational Health Psychology, Vol. 15. London: American Psychological Association.
6. Blom, M., et al., (2009). Daily stress and social support among women with CAD. International Society of Behavioural Medicine. Published online.
7. Brown, W., J., Dobson, A., J., Bryson, L & Byles, J., E. (1999). Journal of Women's Health & Gender-Based Medicine. 8(5): 681-688.
8. Mark 11:23 AMP
9. Perkins, M., (2014), The Age, Tuesday, May 20, pp 4-5.
10. Leaf, C., (2009). Who switched off my brain. Inprov, TX. p15
11. Phil 4:8 NLT
12. Carr, A., (2011) Positive Psychology: The science of happiness and human strengths. Routledge, NY.
13. Weiten, W., (2013). Psychology: themes and variations. Wadsworth Cengage Learning, Canada.
14. Shelley E. Taylor, University of California, LA, https://taylorlab.psych.ucla.edu/wp-content/uploads/sites/5/2014/11/2011_Tend-and-Befriend-Theory.pdf, Retrieved 11th Jul 2015.

15. Weiten, ibid.
16. Weiten, ibid.
17. McCraty, R., Barrios-Choplin, R., Rozman, D., Atkinson, M., Watkins, A., (1997). The impact of a new emotional self-management program on stress, emotions, heart rate variability, DHEA and cortisol. Journal of integrative physiological and behavioural science. pp 151-157.

CHAPTER 2

1. Acts 20:35 KJV21
2. Ps 68:19 NLT
3. Ecc 3:1 NLT
4. Ps 90:4-6 NLT
5. Ps 118:24 NLT
6. Jer 29:11 AMP
7. Heb 11:1 NLT
8. Groeschel, C., (2012), Soul Detox – clean living in a contaminated world. Zondervan, MI.
9. Gal 6:2,5 NIV
10. Cloud, H., & Townsend, J., (1992). Boundaries – when to say yes, when to say no. Zondervan, MI.
11. Ibid
12. Carr, A., (2011) Positive Psychology The science of happiness and human strengths. Routledge, NY.
13. Weiten, W., (2013). Psychology: themes and variations. Wadsworth Cengage Learning, Canada, p220.
14. Hales, D., (1987). How to sleep like a baby. Random House, NY.
15. Gerhman, P., R., Byrne, E., Gillespie, N., & Martin, N., G., (2011). Genetics of insomnia. http://keppel.qimr.edu.au/contents/p/staff/Gehrman_SleepMedClinics_191-202_Jun11.pdf. Retrieved Jan. 2015.
16. Gillespie, N., et al, (2012). Modelling the direction of causation between cross-sectional measures of disrupted sleep, anxiety and depression in a sample of male and and female Australian twins. http://keppel.qimr.edu.au/contents/p/staff/Gillespie_JnlSleep_EPUBJune2012.pdf
17. Gerhman et al, ibid.

18. Ibid.
19. Hales, Ibid.
20. Weiten, Ibid, p220.
21. Hales, Ibid.
22. Weiten, ibid, p222.
23. Kierlin, L., (2008). Sleeping without a pill. Psychiatric Practise, Vol 14(6): 403-7
24. Psalm 4:8 AMP
25. News.bbc.co.uk/2/hi/programmes/happiness-formula/default.stm; Weiten Ibid; Carr Ibid.
26. Neh 8:10NIVUK
27. Unknown author, Bible verse is Psalm 46:10
28. Jam 4:8 NLT
29. Strong, J., (2001). The new Strong's expanded exhaustive concordance of the Bible. Thomas Nelson, TN. (Ref: 7676 & 7673; 5177; 8252).
30. Gen 2:2-3 NLT
31. Strong Ibid, 373; 3062; 2663 & 2664.
32. Strong Ibid, 1515
33. Gal 5:22-23 NLT
34. John 14:27 NLT

CHAPTER 3

1. 2 Tim 3:16
2. Medina, J., (2008). Brain rules: 12 principles for surviving and thriving at work, home, and school, Pear Press, Australia
3. Rom 11:33 NLT
4. Fredrickson, B., L., Cohn, M., A., Finkel, S., M., Coffey, K., A., Pek, J., (2008). Open hearts build lives: Positive emotions induced through loving-kindness meditation, build consequential personal resources, Journal of personality and social psychology, 95 (5), 1045.
5. Wolever, R.Q., (2012) Effective and viable mind-body stress reduction in the workplace. Journal of Occupational Health Psychology, Vol 17.
6. Strong, J., (2001). The new Strong's expanded exhaustive concordance of the Bible, Thomas Nelson, TN. (Ref. G3191)

7. Joshua 1:8 NLT
8. Auerbach, J.E., (2006). Cognitive coaching: Stober, D., R., Grant, A., M., (Editors) Evidence based coaching, Wiley, NJ.
9. 2 Cor 10:5
10. 1 Pet 5:7 CEV
11. Ps 55:22 AMP
12. Ps 31:15 NLT
13. Gal 5:24
14. See Luke 14:33
15. Ps 46:10 NIV
16. Strong Ibid: (Re. H7503)
17. Ibid, (Ref. H3045)
18. Eph 2:6 NLT
19. Phil 4:7
20. Ex 3:14
21. Carr, A., (2011). Positive psychology: The science of happiness and human strengths, Routledge, UK.
22. Ps 23:1-3 NKJV
23. Hart, A., D., (1995). Adrenaline and stress, Nelson, USA.
24. Carr, A., Ibid.
25. Luke 11:33 NLT
26. Gal 5:22-23
27. Paraphrased from Eph 2:10 & Ps 138:8

CHAPTER 4

1. Gal 6:8 the Message
2. John 8:36 NKJV
3. Ps 23:3
4. Pr 31:10 AMP
5. Ps 31:15 MSG
6. Rom 1:16 AMP
7. Beach, S., (2009). The silent seduction for self-talk – Conforming deadly thought patterns to the word of God: Moody, USA.
8. Gen 3:1,4 NLT
9. Beach, Ibid.
10. Meyer, J., (1995). Battlefield of the mind: winning the battle in your mind. Harrison, OK.

11. Leaf, C., Twitter, April, 2013
12. Groeschel, C., (2012). Soul detox – Clean living in a contaminated world. Zondervan, MI.
13. 1 Kin 19:12 AMP
14. Rom 12:2 AMP
15. Rom 12:2 MSG
16. Is 30:15b KJV
17. Matt 14:22, 24, 26, 27 NLT

CHAPTER 5

1. John 10:10
2. Matt 7:20
3. Ps 23:3 AMP
4. Rom 9:18
5. Eph 6:11-12 NIVUK
6. See www.beinhealth.com
7. Wright, H., W., (2009). A more excellent way to be in health. Whittaker, PA. p 16
8. Groeschel, C., (2012). Soul detox – Clean living in a contaminated world. Zondervan, MI.
9. Matt 9:29 NKJV
10. Job 3:25-26 NKJV
11. Matt 6:14 NLTa
12. Ibid., Wright, p 102.
13. Luke 23:34 NIVUK
14. Ten Boom, C., (1974). Tramp for the Lord. Hodder and Stoughton, U.K.
15. Isa 14:12-14
16. Deut 5:7-8 NLT
17. Luke 6:45 NKJV
18. Rom 3:23
19. Matt 7:2-4 CEB
20. Ibid., Groeschel.
21. Deut 5:21 AMP
22. Matt 16:26 NLT
23. Pr 18:14 AMP
24. Jos 1:5; Hebrews 13:5

endnotes

CHAPTER 6

1. Wallis, C., The new science of happiness, Time Magazine April 27, 2009 http://ww.time.com/time/magazine/article/0,9171,1015902,00.html
2. Cohen, S, B., Aspergers test site, http://www.aspergerstestsite.com/30/what-is-aspergers-syndrome/#.UtSUAdKSySo: Retrieved 14/01/14
3. I John 4:16-17
4. 1 Co 13:4-8 NLT
5. Houston, B. (2013). How to maximise your life. Hillsong music, Australia.
6. I John 4:18 AMP
7. Gal 5:22-23 AMP
8. For more information, testimonies, or videos, see beinhealth.org
9. Mattson, M., P., (2005). Energy intake, meal frequency, and health: a neurobiological perspective: Annual Review of Nutrition, Vol. 25: 237-260
10. See Dan 1: 8-16
11. Ps Billie Kennedy, Jan., 30 2014, http://petasoorkia.wordpress.com/
12. Matt 6:9-13
13. YouTube has several clips at http://www.youtube.com/watch?v=IPLVhDDyj4Y&list=PLPxDkHPTkc5LL7xZflhNajYumZlDleUOK
14. Jer 29:11 NIVUK
15. Rom 3:22 NLT
16. Groeschel, C. (2012). Soul detox – Clean living in a contaminated world. Zondervan, MI. p168
17. John 8:11 AMP
18. Groeschel, Ibid.
19. Yerkovich M. & K., (2008). How We Love, Waterbrook Press, CA. pp 291-292.
20. Smith, E. M., (2007). Theophostic Prayer Ministry Manual Revised, New Creation, KY.
21. 2 Cor 12:9 AMP
22. Matt 14:27-29
23. 2 Cor 7:1,9 NLT
24. John 8:3-11

25. I Cor 11:7
26. 2 Cor 5:17
27. 2 Thess 2:16
28. Rom 7:15
29. I John 1:9 AMP
30. Ps 103:3 AMP
31. Jam 5:16 AMP
32. Eph 6:12 KJ21
33. 1 Pet 5:8 AMP
34. Weiten, W., (2013). Psychology: themes and variations, Wadsworth, Cengage Learning, LV.
35. Leaf, C., (2009). Who Switched off my brain, Thomas Nelson, TX.
36. Wright, H. W., A More Excellent Way: Be In Health, GA.
37. Ps 143:3
38. Matt 19:26 UKNIV
39. Eph 6:13
40. John 8:36 NLT
41. See Ps 139: 23-24

CHAPTER 7

1. Ps 139:14 MSG
2. Pr 31:25 AMP
3. Phil 4:7
4. http://www.thefreedictionary.com/beautiful: Retrieved 22nd July 2015.
5. http://www.videosmotivational.com/best-clips/category/womens-empowerment-videos/ Retrieved 20th January 2015.
6. http://www.sermonspice.com/product/49402/karens-story-beauty: Retrieved Youtube 20/01/13
7. Strongs Strong, J., (2001). The new Strong's expanded exhaustive concordance of the Bible. Thomas Nelson, TN. (Ref. H6524)
8. Ps 72:7 NKJV
9. Houston, B., (2013). How to maximise your life: Hillsong Music Australia, Australia.
10. Ibid. p 95
11. Carr, A., (2011). Positive psychology: The science of happiness

and human strengths, Routledge, UK, p15
12. Diener, E., Biswas-Diener, R., (2009). http://internal.psychology.illinois.edu/~ediener/Documents/FS.pdf (see the flourish scale).
13. Rom 12:2 NLT
14. Luke 11:33 AMP
15. 1 Tim 2:8-10 MSG
16. 1 Pet 3:3-4 NKJV
17. http://www.biblegateway.com/resources/ivp-nt/Appropriate-Demeanor-Women
18. Est 2:12-13 NLT
19. Eph 2:10 AMP
20. Pr 31:25-30 CEV
21. Heb 11:1 NLT
22. Ps 45:11 NIV

CHAPTER 8

1. John 17:16-17
2. I Cor 9:22-23 AMP
3. Rucker, Taber, & Harrison, (1981), The effect of clothing variation on first impressions of female job applicants: What to wear when, Social Behaviour & Personality, Vol 9.
4. 1 Sam 16:7 AMP
5. Col 4:6 NLT
6. Luke 11:33 AMP

CHAPTER 9

1. Horgan, A., (2010). Inspirational quotations – loving thoughts for you, Alicat, Australia.
2. Pr 31:30 CEV

ACKNOWLEDGEMENTS

Writing this book was a labour of love but at times excruciating too. I wanted to give up many times (somewhere around draft three... it took eight)! I kept going with the difficult process of editing after the first love affair of getting my original thoughts on paper, because God was on my case.

I was also often reminded that if one beautiful woman somewhere is touched and changed positively as a result of my discomfort, it would be worth it. So for Him and for you, I kept at it. For another day, week, month, year!

Oh and another reason I didn't throw it at the cat or into the rubbish during the five years that this labour of love took, was that my editor simply wouldn't allow it.

If you are reading this, I finished it. Yay! Perhaps you are the woman I wrote it for. And becoming a new un-frazzled and re-dazzled amazing woman of influence!

God bless and see you on the other side, if not before.

Thank you to my God, You are totally awesome. Thank you to my wonderful husband, who stood in the gap many times without (too much) complaint, cooking many meals when I couldn't stop the flow through my fingers to the keyboard. Thanks to our grown up kids who didn't always 'get it' but nevertheless supported me and to our lovely homestay girls who helped in the kitchen when I fell in a heap on the couch after dinner. To Paul, who has always told me the truth in love and to my Senior Pastors, Brian and Bobbie Houston, who show how to love God and people so beautifully. To the most amazing girls on the planet, the AWI team (see www.awomanofinfluence.weebly.com), who are behind me with an incredible vision from God, thank you. To Leigh my editor, I couldn't have done it without your wisdom, advice, sense and the belief that this book needed to be written. Thank you also to the many proof readers, particularly Angela who read and read, and to my mother and sister, who have always believed in me. To Michelle, Karen, Billie, Diane and Kath, you have each exemplified coaching as you have guided me in my journey over many years.

And last but not least, to the women who have allowed me to speak into their lives. I value you and thank you for your trust as I have watched you develop into inspiring women of influence. Without you, this book could not have been written.

Peta Soorkia, 2015

www.ingramcontent.com/pod-product-compliance
Lightning Source LLC
Chambersburg PA
CBHW070600300426
44113CB00010B/1330